You Ask
HE Answers

Swami Tejomayananda

CENTRAL CHINMAYA MISSION TRUST
MUMBAI - 400 072

© Central Chinmaya Mission Trust

First Edition	October	2003	-	2000 copies
Reprint	April	2004	-	1000 copies
Reprint	October	2004	-	2000 copies
Reprint	November	2005	-	2000 copies

Published by:

CENTRAL CHINMAYA MISSION TRUST
Sandeepany Sadhanalaya
Saki Vihar Road,
Mumbai - 400 072, INDIA.
Tel: 91-22-28572367 / 28575806
Fax: 91-22-28573065
Email: ccmt@vsnl.com
Website: www.chinmayamission.com

Distribution Centre in USA:

CHINMAYA MISSION WEST
Publications Division,
560 Bridgetown Pike,
Langhorne, PA 19053, USA.
Tel: (215) 396-0390
Fax: (215) 396-9710
Email: publications@chinmaya.org
Website: www.chinmayapublications.org

Printed by

SAGAR UNLIMITED
28-B, Nand-Deep Industrial Estate,
Kondivita Lane, Andheri Kurla Road,
Mumbai-400 059.
Tel.: 28362777 / 28227699

Price: Rs. 50=00

ISBN 81-7597-215-7

PUBLISHER'S NOTE

This book originally brought out by Chinmaya Mission, New Delhi centre in October 2003 as a souvenir, has generated spontaneous demand for its simplicity of presenting complex spiritual issues in a question-answer from. Chinmaya Mission, New Delhi therefore, deserves appreciation for the initiative taken. CCMT has the pleasure in printing this book again to meet the perennial demand.

April 14, 2004   **Central Chinmaya Mission Trust**
Mumbai

PUBLISHER'S NOTE

This book originally brought out by Chinmaya Mission, New Delhi centre in October 2003 as a souvenir, has generated spontaneous demand for its simplicity of presenting complex spiritual issues in a question-answer from. Chinmaya Mission, New Delhi therefore, deserves appreciation for the initiative taken. CCMT has the pleasure in printing this book again to meet the perennial demand.

April 14 2004   Central Chinmaya Mission Trust
                     Mumbai

FOREWORD

The *Shastras* (Scriptures) are in the form of a dialogue between the Guru and *shishya*; where the latter expresses his doubts through a question. The *Bhagawad Geeta* is one such famous example of knowledge flowing to the student through interaction with the teacher. Some of our well known Upanishads are also revealed as question-answer sessions.

In a systematic study of the *Shastras* the student first has to listen (*shravanam*) and then reflect (*mananam*). This churning process reveals inadequacies or gaps in the understanding of the student. To get firmly rooted in the Knowledge, the student clarifies his or her doubts through direct interaction with the teacher.

The questions and answers in this book have been taken from informal *satsangs* at different times and places. The Delhi Center, on the occasion of a Gyan Yagna has compiled these sessions into a book which has been brought out as a souvenir. I appreciate their efforts and trust this book will serve the purpose of clarifying the doubts of the seeker.

Swami Tejomayananda

CONTENTS

1

SPIRITUAL VISION IS ALL ENCOMPASSING

The quality of our actions and reactions depend upon our vision of life. A narrow vision is divisive. A broad vision is expansive but the supreme vision is all inclusive. The higher the vision, the greater is the mission.

Unless there is a basic change in our vision or value system, we cannot change our lives. Spirituality too is a vision; a vision to understand the oneness of total life. When we comprehend that oneness and are one with the totality, our perspective of life and the world changes.

When people are variously classified as worker, rational, emotional and mystical, their lives are examined only from a particular angle. We are mistaken in concentrating on one factor alone and regarding it as representative of the individual's total life.

Real spirituality involves understanding the totality of life along with the oneness of existence. Often certain rituals are misconstrued as the essence of spirituality. One must understand the meaning of spirituality before one can be expected to behave in a spiritual manner.

Are religion, spirituality and God three different entities?

It depends on the way one perceives the three. When people think of God, they always think of an entity distinct from the real world, dictating terms, rewarding a few and punishing many. A religion is identified by its founder along with specific scriptures, modes of worship and traditions. Spirituality is considered to be the renunciation of the world by a person, who spends the rest of his life meditating in a solitary retreat.

In *Vedanta* and the *Upanishads*, God is defined as, "that which is the Self of all beings", the essence in everything and the support and substratum of the entire universe and not a person or an individual entity.

If you understand religion to mean a set of rituals, it would be distinct from spirituality. But actually, these rituals are only ways of purifying our mind to help us understand concepts of universality or the oneness of life. God, religion and spirituality are not different or isolated entities. They are one and the same.

We have limited ideas about God and religion. We believe all religions are different and impose our faith on others, sometimes even by coercion. *Vedanta* and the *Upanishads* acknowledge no such division. All rituals and practices purify the mind and so are essential to understand the vision of oneself.

Is it possible for a person to be spiritual but not religious?

What you mean by religion is ritualism. Normally we consider one who visits the temple, performs regular worships, says prayers, chants, practices austerities and takes vows like fasting, to be religious. ... A spiritual person is one who pursues Self-knowledge motivated by a longing for Self-realisation. Not just a scholarly or academic pursuit but with a sincere longing to experience the Truth first-hand.

A religious person is one who only does religious activity and may not necessarily be spiritual. Some worship the Lord in an idol but refuse to accept Him in the hearts of all living beings. That is not being spiritual.

Some may have outgrown religious activities as they have served their purpose of preparing the mind. They may be highly spiritual and very sincere in the pursuit of the Truth. Also, some may just not be religiously inclined but still be spiritual.

However, some who practise religious activities are also highly spiritual, as the two are not opposed to each other. Religious activities only aid and intensify our thirst for the Truth.

Can peace of mind be achieved through the development of self dignity, self resolution or auto suggestion?

All these are very helpful but must be geared towards the 'Real Truth'. These qualities can be found in various people in different areas. A good orator does not fear large audiences and a soldier does not fear the battlefield. These people may be very confident in their respective areas of excellence. But we must concern ourselves with the totality of life and be restricted to a particular field to the exclusion of all else.

Thus we constantly return to the theme of total understanding. That is why the *Upanishads* say, "By knowledge alone do we gain liberation". Liberation is freedom from grief, illusion and fear; freedom from slavery to our mind.

It is 'spiritual vision' that is important. Isn't it?

Yes. People have the erroneous belief that spirituality means 'running away from the world' or 'sitting somewhere alone, isolated'. Spiritual vision is all-encompassing, all-inclusive and understands life in its totality.

Iswara satya hai - God is truth. Then will not the things made by Him be *satya* - real?

Yes. But do we call them God's things? No. We call them "our" things. When we interfere in His creation by bringing in "me" and "mine" and "you" and "your", then such a world is *samsara*- fleeting and unreal. If we see the Lord as *satya* - real and the entire world (and oneself) as His, then everything is real. In fact, if we see all as His, all is Him alone and then all is real alone. What therefore is *asat* (unreal) is only our illusions which have to be dispelled.

As long as you quote *Vedanta* as someone else's statements (of the *Guru* or the Scriptures), they are never as efficacious as when you take them, assimilate them and make them your own. Then it is all clear.

What is the role of the *Atma*? What is its function in the face of adversity?

Atma gives sentiency to all inert *upadhis* (instruments). It neither asks a person to do nor stops a person from doing good or bad. This *Atma* which acts through the total mind is called *Ishwara* and when its acts through the individual mind it is called *jiva*. When the *jiva* prays to *Ishwara*, he or she is guided to Self-realization. *Ishwara* plays the role of the *Guru* and leads the *jiva* to righteousness.

How can one find one's *Guru*?

First ask yourself, "Why do we want a *Guru*?" Only when I am suffering from a disease do I need a doctor and look out for one. Similarly, there should first be a longing for Knowledge. Have we realised our bondage? Do we feel the need for Self-knowledge? Then alone is there the need for a *Guru*. Otherwise do not waste your time looking for a *Guru*. The longing for Knowledge also must be all-consuming and intense. It should not just be one of the many casual desires of our life. Then you will find that the law of demand and supply works. It is the job of the Lord to provide you a *Guru*.

Next we may ask, "How can one recognize that 'X' is my *Guru*?" Don't worry. It will happen. I may not know the different nuances of music, but if I have an ear for music, I can recognise a good singer. Similarly, even if I am not spiritually evolved, if I have an earnestness and deep longing, then I will recognise my *Guru*. We are worried about fake *gurus*. Once Gurudev was asked, "I wanted a *Guru*, but found a fake *guru*." He was told, "Your desire for Knowledge must have been fake!"

A fake *guru* will get scared of a very sincere disciple and will not accept him, as his falsehood will get exposed. If the disciple is highly evolved and the *Guru* a noble soul, yet not very advanced spiritually, the *Guru* will tell the disciple, "I can take you this far and no further. You will have to go elsewhere." When we go to an ordinary doctor, he too may say, "Your case requires expert advice. You need to consult another expert. I am not qualified to cure you."

How does one reconcile the fact that there are so many *gurus* and *swamis* often suggesting completely different and seemingly contradictory routes to salvation?

For the same disease one patient decides to go to an allopathic doctor, another to an Ayurvedic doctor, and a third trusts a homeopath. For some people Allopathy may be beneficial, and for others Ayurveda may be more beneficial. So even though there are different kinds of doctors practicing various systems of medicine, who appear to be prescribing different things, the goal is one and the same that the patient should get cured. In the same way, when you have so many different kinds of people with different natures and aptitudes, you need a variety of different methods and spiritual teachers to cater to them all. But the end-goal of peace and happiness remains unchanged.

What does the *Guru* do when he gives *mantra diksha*?

Gurus of the path of *upasana* give *mantra diksha* (whispering *mantras* in the ear, *shaktipata*, etc) to their followers, according to their own sect, in order to enable them to progress towards

Self-realisation. *Gurus* of the path of Knowledge give the wisdom of the *mahavakya*, 'That thou art' and lead the student to Self-knowledge. The success depends on the students aptitude.

One meaning of the word *mantra* is that 'a sound which protects the mind.' It also means 'that which protects when it is reflected upon, by removing the bondage of *samsar* from the seeker.'

How can one handle the *naash* (destruction) of things?

By understanding that there is no *naash* - destruction. There is only seeming *naash* - for nothing can ever be created or destroyed (science has proved this). What is actually happening is not *naash* (destruction) but *naach* (a dance of the change of name and form). It is like the dance of the waves on the sea.

How do we overcome the pain imposed on us, when people say things which hurt us?

Anyone may say anything, but you will feel pain only when you identify yourself as the object of their criticism. And then you react.

There are many ways of responding to such situations. When I am in pain...

a.   I may go on shouting and screaming.

b.   I may also start abusing and inflicting pain on the other person.

c.   I may wonder how to remove my pain, ignoring the other person.

d.   I may lift my mind to higher levels of Truth where these things don't matter at all.

The one who rises above all these is called a *gunatitah*. He is a man of wisdom. Somebody went to a *mahatma* and said, "That lady is talking ill of you." He smiled and said, "She doesn't know me." She came to him and abused him directly. He said, "Who are you talking about? You don't know me. My nature is *sacchidananda*. Whatever you are saying is about this body, its words and actions..."

If someone is talking about a third person, will you feel bad? Keep saying, "I am not the body, mind or intellect. All these properties do not belong to me. He can criticise only these, not the *sacchidananda atma*." Then you will not even be concerned about what he is saying.

The other option is to suffer, cry, complain and then continue again like a child who falls down, cries, dusts himself off and starts all over again. Children fight and then play again. We will react only according to our state of mind, our knowledge and our understanding.

Hinduism believes in one God, one Consciousness that pervades everyone and everything. What is the relationship between this one God which Hinduism believes in and the thousands of deities whom Hindus actually worship?

The power of the government is one, right? But there are many ministers and officers through whom that one power is expressed. In an ocean there are many waves, but all the waves are just different manifestations of the one ocean water. In the same way, there is one God, one infinite power and all the various deities are simply different manifestations of that one power.

Is the Lord's justice really just?

How can we ever know the justice of the Lord? Most of the time, we do not know whether what we do is right or wrong! Also we are totally incapable of knowing what the results of any of our actions will be (though we are free to hope). He alone knows. Fortunately for us He is as compassionate as He is just. If He were merely just, we would have had a much harder time!

2
CHOICE TO ACT — KARMA YOGA

Vyavahara or transaction is of the nature of knowledge and action. We perceive and experience objects through our senses and then we react to the experienced objects. Knowledge is perception and reaction is the response to perception. Perception and response are together called *vyavahara*. If there is a fire somewhere, I will surely respond to it in one way or the other. I may get burnt, I may run away from it, I may try to extinguish it myself, or again I may inform the fire brigade about it. If one feels hungry one does make efforts to appease the hunger. It is impossible to remain without doing anything. As long as life lasts, perception and response will remain. When one is born one has to live. We see that action is inevitable and no one can avoid it.

Our actions, reactions and dealings are determined by our philosophy of life. Even though all creation is one, why is it that each person acts and reacts differently? The reason is that everyone has a different outlook of life. If the vision is correct, there is beauty in action.

How can we know what our duty, or *swadharma*, is?

There are some duties we do not have to go in search of. They come to us automatically according to our designation. For example, we are human beings, so we must live up to the dignity of being human.

Our first duty is to take care of those who are below us, or in a lower state. Among brothers, the elder must protect the younger one. We should take care of those who are less fortunate or less evolved, whether they are birds, animals, other creatures, plants or trees. This is our first duty. But today we find strong people destroying those who are weaker, the rich exploiting the poor etc. This is wrong.

When born in a family the child automatically gains a certain identity. As a child one's duty is to obey one's parents and serve them. In school and college, as a student, one must study. This is one's duty according to his /her status. In a job one has a designation, where the post, duties and responsibilities are clearly assigned. These duties are all known to us. Our problem is that we do not do them. So when a difficult situation comes, we do not understand it.

The second category of duty is a little different. This is in accordance with your aptitude. *Brahmana dharma, kshatriya dharma* etc., refer to these categories of people. We must discover our aptitude and choose that field of activity to which we are best suited. For example, if a person is an artist by temperament, that is his *swadharma*. If he pursues it, he will enjoy it, succeed and contribute to the field of art. But where is the money in art? So he is advised to become a doctor, businessman etc. If he switches to some other profession, he is not doing his duty. He may continue to pursue art as a hobby, but he may never shine as an artist. One must pursue that field for which one has the aptitude (even if dissuaded by other people), because one will shine in one's *swadharma*.

If we accept the *karma* theory, and resign ourselves to our so called fate, are we not adopting a fatalistic attitude? Does this help an individual in a positive manner?

If what we get is the result of our *karma* where does fatalism come in? Who performed the *karma* in the first place? We, is it not? If we suffer because of bad *karma*, can't we compensate now? Suppose we overeat, we can either say it is our *karma* and suffer or cure ourself with medication and lead a healthier life.

Once we understand that our suffering is because of our *karma*, we can undo it.

Is there a hope for a better deal in the next *janma* (lifetime)?

People generally have erroneous notions about *karma phala* (fruit of action). Whenever an action is performed, it is followed by a result in the physical sense, but this result may not be instantaneous.

If, on a visit to someone else's house, one entertains the evil thought of stealing something, agitation begins immediately. As a direct result of the thought, the mind is restless. This restlessness however does not persist if the thought is banished from the mind. Again, the results are immediate. Now, if the thought is allowed to flourish and the individual steals, he / she may not be caught and punished instantly, but is sure to be apprehended sooner or later. But the feelings of guilt and fear will remain from the time the object has been stolen. Our ideas regarding the results of our actions are thus flawed and at fault.

People have yet to grasp the concept of *karma* and rebirth. They have perhaps understood half the truth but believe they know it all.

Our *vasanas* may be such that they turn us towards spirituality. If we don't have such spiritual *vasanas* what chance do we have to evolve?

We are not slaves to our *vasanas*. We have control over them. We can direct our thoughts into purifying channels through *satsang* and thereby evolve.

Destiny is determined by *vasanas* because *vasanas* drive us to act in a particular way and the results of these actions become our destiny. Is free will also influenced by our *vasanas*?

Vasanas (our tendencies) drive us to *karma*, which in turn leads to *phala*. This is otherwise called our destiny. However free will is not a product of *vasanas*. It is a human right, a special quality exclusive to human beings. How we use free will may be influenced by our *vasanas*. So we can use your free will well or otherwise. At the end of the *Geeta*, Lord Krishna says to Arjuna, "*Yathecchasi tatha kuru* - do as you think fit."

If we feel we still cannot be sure that we can use our free will well, surrender it to God, as Arjuna did (with the words, "*Karishye vachanam tava* - I shall do as You say"). Since He has said, "*Teshaam aham samudharta* (I redeem them)," tell God, "Please lead my life for me". However we must also keep in mind the fact that this kind of total surrender is the greatest *purushartha* and it is very difficult.

Is destiny more powerful or human effort?

If we are convinced that destiny is more important, then we should accept that every success or failure that comes our way is because of our destiny. On the other hand if we believe that self-effort alone is important, then too there is no problem, because we will accept responsibility for all our failures and successes. But if we believe that both are important, a problem arises because we will not be able to say with certainty how much of our success or failure is due to self-effort and how much due to destiny. Probably we would then end up saying that everything that happened over which we had no control happened because of destiny and the rest was due to self-effort. However, the best thing is to know that in a given situation we are only required to act to the best of our ability and knowledge and leave the rest. If the result is pre-ordained, then the question that comes up is, pre-ordained by whom? If it is by us, then try to change it. If we cannot change the result, then try to change the state of mind. When we know our true Self then there is no question of self-effort or destiny because we would then have realized that the entity as a *jiva* itself is illusory.

What is destiny and how does it control us? What is self-effort?

What we get in the present is our destiny. What we do with what we get is our self-effort. Each moment in life we find that we are faced with one situation or the other. We do not know how it comes, why or from where. We do not know exactly how much we have contributed to bring about this situation before us. The fact that there is a situation, leads to the conclusion that it must have one or more causes. The important thing is that we must know how to deal with it with a cool mind, in a way which uplifts and is beneficial to all concerned. Even though we have no control over how to deal with it, we may do it one way or the other or not do anything at all. *Sant Eknath* had a supportive wife; so he thanked God for the same. *Sant Tukaram* had a cantankerous wife who opposed him all the time. He too thanked God for a wife like that which prevented him from getting attached. Each of them dealt with their destiny in a positive way.

Some say that even our responses to situations are not self-effort, but destined. That belief too should not cause problems, as, then we would have no complaints. We would accept things as they come, cheerfully.

Some say that there is no destiny or self-effort. It is all the will of God. Then also we accept all situations as the gifts of God.

Some others feel - we create the situation and we respond to it; we are totally responsible. This attitude also can lead us to a positive response to situations as, we do not blame anyone else, learn to be responsible, and are careful in our responses.

Is it possible to perform action both for self-interest and as a duty towards God at the same time?

There is self-interest in everything we do. It cannot be avoided. Without it we don't do anything. So what do we mean when we say, "Perform actions selflessly"?

Self-interest can be of many kinds. At the lowest level, it is only in terms of material gains. Is there any money in it? Will it give us power or pleasure? Generally, at this level there are only these three considerations. If our self-interest is of this kind alone, then it will always come in conflict with the other person, because he also wants money, power and pleasure. In the beginning, when a person has not matured much, the *Shastras* say, "Okay, there is nothing wrong with these interests, but at least adopt such means which will not harm others. Work hard, fulfill your duties and enjoy yourself." There is self-interest, but in an acceptable form.

As we grow further, we still want something for ourselves, but our horizon expands and we don't want it *only* for ourselves. This is a mixture - what will we get and what can we give? This is progress towards realisation. We get money, but give 10% of it in charity. Earlier we wanted the entire 100% of it and the other man's portion as well! At least now, we have started thinking about what we can give. So here we have self-interest, but we also think of and give others.

In the third stage of evolution, we think of what we will get, but more in terms of spiritual wealth than material wealth. Will what we get purify our mind? Will it create love for God in our hearts? Will it be conducive for gaining Knowledge? Even when people join spiritual organisations, there is some expectation of gain. That is why all of you come here. But the gain here is in terms of Knowledge and a chance to serve. So there is a combination of self-interest and selflessness.

However, the idea of self-interest goes on changing. Further up on the ladder, there are people who give up all their material things and feel great joy inside. But that joy is also a form of self-interest alone. There is no action where self-interest is not involved - only the idea of self-interest becomes more and more refined. A person's highest demand is Realisation through purification.

Here is an interesting point. In the case of a material gain, say, the post of a prime minister, or even that of a company director, for one post there will be many candidates. Only one will get it and hence there is conflict between them. But the gain of God is wonderful indeed! There may be hundreds of seekers, all of them wanting God. Still there will be no conflict because each one can get God and each one can get Him completely. All rivers want the ocean, all of them go into it and all of them become the ocean. There is no scope for cut-throat competition or jealousy.

How can one know if he is performing an action for the Lord alone or whether he is holding back a little, just convincing himself that it is for the Lord's sake and there is some self-interest behind it after all?

The answer to this question can be given only by you. The most important thing is sincerity. If a person is really sincere and genuine, he will know if the action was actually done selflessly as everyone sees it and believes it or whether there was some ego and self-interest involved.

However, there is an indication which can point out the truth of the matter. If a person has performed the action only for the sake of the Lord, his or her mind will be at peace. It will be in a happy state regardless of what the world may say or do. There will be no agitation or uneasiness. But if there is pretence (knowingly or unknowingly), there is already expectation of recognition and approval of the action. If there is no appreciation, there is agitation. In the face of criticism of the action, there will be unhappiness and the individual will react violently, because actually it was not done selflessly. If the action is selfless, criticism will leave the person unmoved. It will not make any difference because he or she does not want to prove anything.

A man knowledgeable in the Scriptures, approached the great Kabirdas. He was itching to have an argument with him on scriptural matters. Wanting to prove to him and others that he knew the *Shastras* better, he challenged Kabir to a scriptural debate. Kabir asked, "Why?" "Because I want to defeat you," he said. "That's all? Then I accept my defeat," he added, "I certify you the winner". Kabir knew the Truth. He did not want to argue about it. If someone wants to argue, it is permitted, but we do not have to prove any point. If we are devoted to God, why do we want to prove it to this world? If God knows it is enough and the mind is at peace, there are no complaints, no anger.

It would be very boring to come into this world again and again and do the same thing. I would like to make this my last birth. But will I have to come back if I kill mosquitoes and insects?

If the present life is boring, then future lives are also imagined to be boring. Some say, first thing in the morning, "Good morning God!", whilst some others say, "Good God! Morning......!" Normally our life is a routine and drudgery, interspersed with enforced thrills. There is really not much meaning and purpose to live by or for. No wonder we do not want such a repeat performance.

However, devotees of the Lord say, "I am not interested in *dharma*, wealth, pleasures or even birth and death. O Lord, I do not mind taking birth in any form, any number of times, as long as I am able to worship Your feet or have devotion in my heart." *Hanumanji* refused to go to *Saket Loka* (the Lord's abode) and said that he would rather stay on earth and find fulfillment in listening to and spreading the glories of the Lord.

About killing mosquitoes and the like, keep the environment clean in the first place. Most insects really do not harm us. Leave them alone. They go away on their own. Ants are busy doing their own things, silently and unobtrusively. Why kill them? If, however, they are harmful insects, which spread diseases etc., you can kill them. We are asked to do *praayaschit* - (expiatory acts) or pray to seek forgiveness for unintentionally harming or killing other beings like insects. We should avoid doing so intentionally. Actually, more harmful than the outside insects and worms, are the ones in our heart like anger, jealously, greed etc. Why don't we concentrate on them?

Baba Gangadas was once resting under a tree during his travels. There were many mosquitoes around and he could not sleep even though he was very tired. He prayed to God, "O Lord, if I am unable to wake up, tomorrow You will not get your *pooja*". The mosquitoes mysteriously disappeared!

The 32nd verse of the ninth chapter of the *Geeta* says, "Hey Arjuna! Even those born of sinful wombs, women, *vaishyas* and *shudras* who take refuge in Me, attain liberation". Please explain.

To understand this verse, the subject matter of the ninth chapter should be understood. In the beginning the Lord says, "I will give you that Knowledge, knowing which you will get liberated." After presenting the Knowledge, He says, "Those who are devoted to Me get liberated." If only those who are highly qualified get liberated, then what about sinners? The Lord assures, "Even if a great sinner turns his mind to Me, he gets liberated". Now, here He assures us that even those less qualified or in some way handicapped, can get liberated if they turn to Him.

In all religions, some orthodox people propagate the view that only a chosen few attain liberation or go to heaven. They also feel that only some have the right to worship the Lord. Here the Lord removes such wrong notions. All have a right to worship and attain Him. This verse is not meant to discriminate against classes of people or as a slur towards them. It only shows that the Lord, out of compassion, overlooks our handicaps when we surrender to Him and remember Him in single-pointed devotion.

a. *Paapa yoni* - animals, birds, etc. are referred to, here, as those born of sinful wombs. Sin is that which creates an obstacle in the path of our spiritual progress. Sleep by itself is not a sin, but sleeping in a spiritual discourse or during meditation is! Animals do not have the capacity to discriminate between the Real and unreal. This faculty is essential for Self-realisation. However, by the grace of the Lord, even they have attained liberation, e.g. Jatayu, Hanuman, Gajendra etc.

b. *Stri* - women. Women have always been discriminated against from ancient times and even at present in the most advanced countries this continues. Here by women, Bhagawan implies those with a sentimental nature and those who get attached too easily. Such people find it difficult to gain Self-realisation, be they men or women. Many great women have attained Self-realisation.

c. *Vaishya* - business class. A person with a profit-making attitude does not get far in spiritual life. A businessman asked a saint, "What will I get if I take the name of the Lord daily?" The saint said, "Get out! You can't even take the Lord's name without a profit motive!"

d. *Shudra*- labour class. Here one who is unrefined is implied. All of us are born *shudras*. Manners, etiquette, culture, education etc. are given to us as we grow. An unrefined person too can attain the highest spiritual Knowledge, if he or she, with all sincerity, turns to the Lord.

After total surrender, what does one do?

If you can truly totally surrender, then it is for God to do, not you! The problem is that we do not totally surrender. The greatest *purushartha* (act of free will) of a *sadhaka* (seeker) is true and total surrender. If that is done, the individual's *purushartha* ends and God's will takes over.

Please explain what is 'swadharma' and 'paradharma'.

Swadharma means one's own *dharma* and *paradharma* means another's *dharma*. We will see what they mean from three standpoints. First the highest level.

a. *Dharma* means nature.

It is that which is inherent and cannot be given up or taken on. Our own true nature is *Sat-Chit-Ananda* (Existence-Consciousness-Bliss). To abide in one's own nature is called 'following *swadharma*.' To consider ourselves as the body-mind-intellect and live as them is called *paradharma*. To think I am fat, tall, fair etc., or sad, glad and so on, or intelligent, talented, etc., is *paradharma*. Following *paradharma* brings sorrow and is fraught with fear (*paradharmo bhayaavahah*- *Geeta* ch. 3).

b. *Dharma* means duties.

Each one of us has duties which come to us unasked, depending on the status, post, place that we are in, e.g. a student's duty is to study. To do one's own duty is *swadharma* and to do another's is *paradharma*. In settling a land dispute, an evaluator is called in court. His job is to evaluate the land and not pass judgment as to whom it should belong to. A clerk's duty may be to write cheques. He cannot sign them in the absence of his boss or forge his boss's signature.

c. *Dharma* means one's own inherent aptitude.

To pursue one's own inherent aptitude is *swadharma* and that of another is *paradharma*. Suppose a young boy, very gifted in music, is forced by his parents to become a businessman. He may make a lot of money as a businessman, but may not find great fulfillment. On the other hand, if he becomes a musician, he would rapidly excel in his field and also find great joy and satisfaction.

Are all actions in our life the result of past actions?

This is only partially true. The circumstances, the period in which we are born and our present nature depends on our past actions. But what we do with the present condition is entirely in our hands. There is neither complete freedom nor complete dependence in the world.

3
COMMON SENSE IS ALL YOU NEED

Despite the awareness that all religions teach the same thing, we are painfully aware of the differences and divisions. The various experiences of life show that we want to live happily, collectively and together. A little thinking shows that the only thing required for this is common sense! For applying or using common sense in life, we do not have to belong to any particular philosophy or religion. Speaking on this rare phenomenon, Swami Vivekananda opined, "Common sense is the most uncommon thing in this world!"

First we must understand that we are born in this world and we have to live our own life. It is not possible to live the life of another person. Primarily we must take responsibility for our life and secondly learn to mind our own business. For happiness two things are necessary, first we have to change and second we have to live in peace and harmony with the world around. There is no substitute for this. We all want to live happily and do not want anyone to cause us sorrow by cheating, looting, plundering or betraying us. Since we do not want anyone to destroy our happiness, should we not show consideration for theirs? The one great lesson I have learnt from my experiences is, **"Look at everyone as yourself but do not consider everyone like yourself."**

How relevant can scriptures written thousands of years ago be in the 21st century?

The nature and cause of the world and the reality behind it has not changed over the years! Man is almost the same now as he was then in terms of his likes and dislikes, anger, ambitions, frustrations, love, struggle etc. All the Scriptures talk about man and his struggle. Therefore, they are as relevant today as they were then, in fact more so. Today we find that man's problems have multiplied, while his freedom has decreased.

Some sceptics argue that India has seen more religious Masters than any country in the world and yet we have so many social, political and communal problems. How do you explain this?

It is because we have so many problems that we need so many Masters! You see those people who have followed the teachings of the Scriptures and the Masters have attained nobility and peace. It is not the Scriptures or the Masters that will change the world, but whether people follow their teachings or not.

Medical science has become so well developed. Yet why is there so much disease and illness even in the most advanced countries? Those who live clean lives and take their medicines are fine. But those people who do not follow a sensible diet and live totally unnatural lives are more prone to falling ill. It is not the fault of medical science! It depends on whether people choose to follow medical science or not.

Nowadays many people mechanically go to temples, pray and perform a few rituals - but the spirit of religion and what religious Masters have been saying is not being followed. That is why there are problems.

If all the saints have the same philosophy then why is there no harmony in society?

The countless people in society being at different levels of spiritual evolution cannot have the same knowledge. Even saints have a past life. They too were not the same. The requirement is that whosoever understands the importance of righteous living should put forth effort to live in that way. The whole society cannot get transformed at the same time. That itself is its uniqueness.

How can we analyse our spiritual growth?

Supposing we are unwell. How do we know that we are getting well? When symptoms of the disease recede and signs of good health return, we know that we are getting better. For example, the headache and nausea is not there. Though the weakness remains but the appetite and mobility are returning… and so on.

Similarly, we understand that we are spiritually growing:

a. When worldliness decreases, when worldly matters don't matter so much, when we are able to maintain a mental poise even in adversity and when insults, obstacles, praise or pleasures do not make us dejected or elated. In short, when dispassion towards the world increases.

b. When our appetite for spirituality increases, when we long for *satsang*, look forward to our regular spiritual practices, wait for the study class, are full of joy and enthusiasm for spiritual activities - like a lover awaits his/her dates, we await our date with the Lord - then we are progressing spiritually.

Rama Raksha Stotra has a lovely verse which means 'I salute that Shri Rama on whose left side is Sitaji and on the right is Lakshmana and in the front sits Hanumanji.' Shri Rama symbolises Knowledge and discrimination, Sitaji devotion, Lakshman dispassion, and Hanumanji selfless service. When all four qualities reside in the heart, we are progressing.

Spirituality should not remain an activity. It should become one's life, effortless and natural, like breathing. It should become one's very nature and vision.

Children are born with their own *vasanas* and with their own *karmaphalas* to exhaust. What is the role of parents in their upbringing?

The role of the parents is to give their children a sense of direction and create an atmosphere so that the building of wrong tendencies is avoided. They should remember that children have their own *karmas* to exhaust and must therefore raise them without worrying unduly about them. If children go totally astray, there is an excuse for worrying. Otherwise, parents should allow them to grow at their own pace.

In our job, we may have to exaggerate the truth in order to get a bank loan or manipulate accounts. If we do not, we may lose the job. What is our duty? To support the company and family or do what is morally right?

The questioner already knows the answer. The answer is to follow the path of righteousness - *dharmam cara*.

a. Desirelessness allows us to uncompromisingly follow righteousness in life. What if we have desires? The Scriptures then teach us to manage our desires.

b. Fulfill those desires which are unopposed to righteousness or *dharma*. What is *dharma*? That which integrates us within and without is *dharma*. The opposite is *adharma*. To eat while hungry is our body's *dharma*, but to overeat is *adharma*. To earn money to sustain oneself and the family is *dharma* but to have unending greed for money is *adharma*.

c. Fulfill legitimate desires by legitimate means. To desire to buy a TV by earning is not wrong, but by robbing is.

d. Put a limit even to the fulfillment of legitimate desires. In fulfilling our desires we tend to multiply them or get caught in them. We create artificial needs, want to gratify ourselves endlessly, and keep everyone happy. Thus we never grow out of desires. The idea of fulfilling desires is to slowly go beyond them. If we are attached to childhood toys even in old age, there is something wrong! Each householder must decide that he/she will one day become a *sanyaasin* i.e., renounce all. Anyway, in death we have to give up everything. This thought will prevent us from getting too attached, and from increasing our needs.

e. Only under extraordinary circumstances should we compromise with our values. The best solution, however, is to live uncompromisingly. But if external pressures and the system are such, we may have to compromise. This compromise should not be out of greed. It should not be to such an extent that we lose all self-respect or turn criminal.

Some turn self-righteous and start calling others sinners and bad people. Some keep blaming others for their compromises. That is not right. We alone are responsible for our actions. If a person lives a life of *dharma*, others soon realise that he/ she will not compromise; so after some initial trouble, they are left alone. Hence one must live a life of righteousness.

How can one work with dedication to the Lord while doing duties one doesn't like?

Once we say 'duties', don't label them as pleasant or unpleasant. In duty the question of like or dislike does not arise. You can not say, "I like hiring people but not firing them!" If the position is such that both these jobs have to be done, then we must do them without any feelings of like or dislike. If one remembers the altar of dedication, then these things will not count.

We know what happened to Arjuna. He did not like his duty, and his dislike prompted him to leave the battlefield. Bhagawan then said, "If you are going away because of your aversion, it is not the right thing to do. You must stay and fight because it is your duty." The very definition of duty is 'that which has got to be done'. So we have to remain firm in it whether we like it or not.

How do we know that we are giving charity to the right person?

The important thing is to make sure we give with *shraddha* (faith), not without. Initially if it matters and one wants to be sure that one is giving to the right person, the worth of the receiver may be ascertained. After giving charity, essentially one should feel peaceful. But if the action leaves one more agitated wondering whether or not one is doing the right thing, then there is something wrong. So, initially give only the charity that gives a good feeling. Once mental purity increases and there is spiritual maturity, the questioning will automatically stop. For, to give alone is ours - what is done with what we give is the receiver's problem.

Another interesting view point which is seldom considered is - when we give, we want to test the worth of the receiver. This is surely a one-way analysis, because when someone gives us money/ praise/prostration, do we ever question our own worthiness to receive? Remember to keep this in mind too!

Please suggest some methods by which one may remain focused on the Lord while performing actions.

If it is just physical work, a method can be prescribed. If I am asked, "How to clean this hall?" I would say, " Use a broom or a vacuum cleaner or employ somebody." There are alternate methods which can be suggested because it is physical thing. But dedication is an attitude; it comes by right understanding. How can we gain this attitude?

Suppose someone applies for a job in a private company or in a government office, what would they expect of the employee? Simple, that he/she must work for them. However, in the job instead of working for the company, the employee starts misusing that power and authority to collect money only for him or herself or joins hands with a rival company and starts working against the employers. What would be the consequences? The employee would simply but surely be dismissed. When a job, a designation, a status or money are given, we are expected to work for them. To that source from which we derive all our powers, we must dedicate everything. This is the principle.

From birth onwards we have been given the faculties of the sense organs, the mind, the intellect and the body. How many different kinds of powers and abilities have been given to us! Without these, nobody would even have given us a job.

We can see, hear, taste, smell, talk, think, feel, act - from where did we get all these? Did any government or private company give them to us? Did we buy them in the supermarket? No, we were blessed with these from birth. Just think a person who merely employs us and gives us a little money expects that we should work for him/her. Not only that, they expect our loyalty as well. The Lord, in His infinite kindness has given us all these equipments - isn't it our duty to dedicate them to Him alone?

Hence we chant the *sloka*:

> *kayena vaca manasendriyairva*
> *buddhyatmana va prakrterswabhan at*
> *karomi yadyat sakalam parasmai*
> *narayanayeti samarpayami*

I dedicate all my *karmas*, all that I do with my body, mind, senses, intellect, to Narayana. I offer Him these powers and abilities.

Once we become thus aware, dedication is natural. In a democratic set-up, when we vote leaders to power, we expect them to work for us, for the country. Any politician or minister who remembers this will become everybody's beloved.

We owe our very existence to *Paramatma*. This Awareness, this Knowledge is the only method by which we can remain focused. If we forget this, no other exercise we do can be of any use.

We are often unable to decide what our duty is. For Arjuna, Krishna was available. Some people may have advisers. If a person is totally unaware of all this and no one is there to guide him, what will he do?

Life is such that even when such a situation arises, whether we have professional advice or not, we have to take decisions to the best of our ability or understanding. How does a person who is unaware and has no adviser take decisions?

Firstly one fixes one's identity and in accordance with that the duties. Take for example the case of a subordinate being asked by the boss to do something. He/she does not know whether to do it because it may appear that the boss is not asking for the right thing. In such an eventuality how should one decide?

The employee may think, "I am only a subordinate, he is my boss. Why should I unnecessarily think too much about it? He has told me to do it; I will." That is one way. Or he may think, "I am a responsible person also. If I protest and resist, he may give me an adverse official report. I may be demoted or suspended, I have a family…" If the thinking is, "I am a subordinate or householder," the individual will do as he/she is asked to do.

On the other hand, if one sees oneself as an individual, a responsible citizen or a spiritual seeker, the thinking will be, "I will not do this even if I have to resign my job." The decision will depend on one's understanding or maturity and one's identification as householder, citizen etc. It is possible that the choice is made without so much philosophical analysis!

Sometimes consequences of the decision may be correct and sometimes they may be painful and cause trouble. One learns from experience and thus life goes on. Even if we get professional advice, because it goes against our desires, often we do not follow it.

God is seated in our hearts. Seek Him, sincerely pray to Him and ask Him for His guidance. If we are sincere, He will surely guide us from within.

It is said that our conscience is the "Voice of God". But how do we know that it is not just our own mind playing tricks?

If we are honest with ourselves we will know whether it is the 'Voice of God' or our own mind playing tricks. Generally, the first voice is our Conscience. The second thought or the interpretation of the first thought is usually our mind. Sometimes a thought comes, "I must give Rs. 10,000/- in charity." Thereafter the mind starts thinking, "Why now, why so much, Rs. 5000/- is enough" etc. In many situations the conscience warns us, "Don't do this. It will harm you." Thereafter the mind finds excuses, "This is a human weakness. I am after all human. I will do it only once", etc.

Sometimes, whilst indulging in negative activities we do not feel bad, as we have asked our conscience to shut up. But after doing what our conscience has asked us not to do, we experience fear, regret, shame, tension etc. These reactions will show whether we followed the 'voice of our conscience' or the dictates of our mind. If that is not understood, then, blows from the outside world will definitely make us understand this.

We want to renounce. But it is so tough!

Hasten slowly! In family life, first, involve in as much *satsang* as possible, without it interfering too much with family duties. At the same time, do not get too involved while performing duties. For instance, there may be certain unavoidable functions (like a wedding) that one is invited to. One must attend, but there is no need to sit there for hours finding out too much about unnecessary things. Shorten phone calls and such tendencies to waste time (or rather kill time!) Thus slowly create more time for involvement in *Vedanta*. With proper time management, one will gradually find much more time for the spiritual path. As the seeker's sincerity increases, grace also flows to make this possible.

Can spiritual exercises do anything to alleviate our physical suffering, especially in the case of incurable diseases of the body?

It is worth asking what the cause of our physical diseases is. More often than not we ourselves create the cause. Many toxins are built up in our body and this leads to diseases. With the normal course of treatment, more chemicals are injected into the body. Despite all this, sometimes the situation only worsens. Once I met a lady in Pune, who told me that one fine day, she woke up to find that she could not open her eyes at all. She consulted an eye-specialist, who considered the situation and suggested injections, but he was doubtful if they would really help. She then consulted a naturopath she knew. He asked her to eat only raw vegetables for the next two weeks. Believe it or not, at the end of the given period, her eyes opened, without any medicines or injections. I have heard a similar story of a lady who was cured of cancer in the same way. She lived in Vinoba Bhave's *ashram* in Paunar for a few years, eating only raw vegetables and avoiding all cooked food. Finally, there was no trace of cancer. Usually, for cancer, doctors prescribe toxic medicines, radiation etc. Here we find that even at a physical level, meeting someone with an understanding of Nature's ways can help us.

Spiritually, a lot of help is available. It is said that the mind rules over the body. Spiritual exercises, Knowledge and practices can strengthen our mind. If the mind says, "I am going to get well," even that will have an effect. Secondly, even if the body is sick with an incurable disease, the mind can be lifted and tuned to a higher Truth. Then the disease will not affect us to the same degree. An example will make this clear. Walking in the hot sun, holding an umbrella over one's head, one is protected from the scorching heat, though the heat of the sun is not reduced or removed. In the same way, spiritual and devotional practices create an umbrella over us. In the language of devotion, it is called the umbrella of the Grace of God. The troubles remain, but they do not affect us so much. Sri Ramakrishna Paramahamsa and Ramana Maharshi both suffered from cancer. But their minds were so immersed in the Truth that they could say, "If there is disease in the body, let it be there…" So we should do spiritual *sadhana* not only because we are sick, but because spiritual *sadhana* can give us real health.

In life we meet some people with whom we just don't click. But the Lord is there in them too. How can we serve them?

Before we decide whether we like a person or not, find out whether he/she has a problem with us. If not, and if he/she needs help, do it. However if it is a mutual animosity, then it is best to avoid each other physically. If that is not possible (may be he/she is a close family member), at least try to keep a mental distance. Why fall on people who do not want us? Pray for them - that is the best service we can do for them, as they do not want to have anything to do with us.

At the same time maintain a proactive attitude. Try not to be reactive. Whenever saints are insulted or criticised, they remain quiet continuing with their work. In time, people realise their error and beg forgiveness. But even if they do not, it does not matter to the *mahatma*.

How can we correct others?

Do not try to correct others unless they are open to advice. We can only lead our own life - we can never lead another's life. It is best to keep to oneself (a polite way of saying 'mind your own business!') This may sometimes be construed as selfishness. But who is not selfish? We all start off by being selfish. The only thing we should make sure is that our selfishness or self-interest does not interfere with another's path or life.

In this context, remember the Serenity Prayer - "God, grant me the serenity to accept the things I cannot change, courage to change the things I can, and wisdom to know the difference". For this we need *viveka* (discrimination).

Our job is to purify our mind. Through a pure mind, discrimination is born. Then one will know where to speak and where not to, what to do and what not to, etc.

How should we look at our family?

We can use our circumstances to grow internally. Do not keep waiting for His grace but see it in everything. A devout man was once caught in the middle of a river in a leaking boat. He believed that the Lord would surely come to his rescue. A man offered to throw down a rope from a bridge above. The sinking man said that he would rather wait for God's grace. A passing ship offered help which again the man refused, waiting for God's help. Sure enough, the boat sank and with it the man. In heaven, he questioned God in great disillusionment, "I trusted You, and You never came to me when I needed You most!" God answered, "Of course I did. Twice! Once I came as the man from the bridge and once as the captain of the nearby ship. What could I do when you refused My help?"

See every happening in life as proof of His grace. For instance, serve your mother with *matru devo bhava* (look upon her as God, as is said in our Scriptures). Also maintain the same approach with other members of the family. At the same time, when a family member dies, we must pray with all our heart for his/her happiness, mourn a while if one has to, but in time, also accept it as freedom from one more bondage, to enable one to dedicate one's life more to God. At the same time, never wish that anyone is not there! So when they are there, serve them seeing the Lord within them. When they are not, see that too as an opportunity to grow further.

How can we convince others to come to *yajnas* or reap the benefits that accrue from the Knowledge of Vedanta?

It is better not to try and convince anybody. Invite them to come to the *yagnas* through good publicity. Then leave it to them to decide. One may ask, "Why all this publicity? It attracts so few. Of these few how many really listen and how many really follow the teaching?" Is it not the same with all advertisements for products? The purpose of repeatedly airing the advertisement for 'Saridon' is not to make us buy it now but to ensure that the brand name stays in the mind. So when one gets a headache (which we might, even by hearing the advertisement so many times!) we will remember Saridon first.

Here too the idea is not only to make people come to *yajnas* but to keep the idea of *Vedanta* in their minds. We attempt to let people know that such spiritual guidance is available. If they feel the need for it sometime, we are there for them.

There are certain rituals like '*shraaddha*' which only men can perform. Why not women? Why the discrimination?

Women should be happy that they do not have to do it. Why should they feel discriminated against? The constitution enjoins duties for different people in different posts. Person X does not ask why he/she cannot do Y's duties. This does not imply discrimination against anyone. It is the way the constitution is drafted to facilitate the smooth running of the government. Similarly, the Scriptures say that men can do certain actions; women cannot. Accept it. It is for our own good.

4
RISE THROUGH RIGHT ACTION

In the *Bhagawad Geeta, Sri Krishna* describes how three types of persons, with three different visions live in the world. A person with a *sattwic* vision lives in bliss and freedom because he/she perceives the oneness of things and beings and, therefore, the heart is filled with love for all. The *rajasic* person is constantly struggling seeing differences, which create divisions, likes and dislikes in the mind. The *tamasic* person lives in bondage, taking the part for the whole and getting fanatically attached to one little thing.

The majority of people belong to the second category. They are always craving and longing for the results of action. For them, *happiness is based on the result of the action.* Everyone will agree that we want happiness and we want it now and forever. But, our way of living and thinking is such that we always say, "If I get this object, then I will be happy," or, "I am doing this to get a specific result to be happy." We keep postponing our happiness for the future: If I pass the examination, I will be happy; if I get that job, I will be happy; if I am able to go to another country, I will be happy. If I get married, I will be happy"…and so on. Thus man is always preparing himself to be happy - he's never happy!

Look at the contradiction - we want happiness now but are postponing it to the future by making it dependent on the result. So firstly, our happiness will be in the future and secondly, since the future is very uncertain, our happiness is also uncertain. But suppose, we enjoy the very action itself, the essential point is that an action is always performed in the present - an action cannot be performed in the past or future. *So if our joy is in the action itself, then our joy is in the present.* And since the action is in our hands; it is within our reach and there is no uncertainty about it either.

We have the choice to perform an action but once it is performed, the result is not in our control, as it is dependent on many other factors. Thus, happiness is fleeting, uncertain and in the future, for a person obsessed with the results of his/her actions. Such a person becomes extremely greedy; there is no end to one's desire for more and life becomes a relentless, futile struggle for happiness.

Is there any benefit from a ritual which is done without understanding its meaning or purpose?

While the greatest benefit can be obtained from rituals only when they are done with proper understanding, rituals done mechanically can also bring smaller benefits by way of self-discipline.

Hindu philosophy provides escapism for the old. Why is it not targeting itself to the young at the school level?

Hindu philosophy never advocates escapism to anyone. Did the *Bhagawad Gita* provide escapism to Arjuna? In fact, Hinduism helps us not to escape from life but to face it with courage. It gives us a total vision of life. Perhaps the right word to use here is not escapism but 'refuge' because Hinduism provides refuge to all. So far as targeting children is concerned, organizations like Chinmaya Mission have been conveying the essence of Hindu philosophy to them through forums like Balvihars (classes for children).

In *samsaric* life, Self-realization is impossible. So why does Hinduism not insist on celibacy?

The word '*samsar*' as used in Hinduism is not to be confused with getting married and having children. '*Samsar*' means the bondage of worldly life. To consider oneself as the physical body is the source of all our problems. With such identification, Self-realization is impossible. All celibates are not free from *samsaric* bondages. What is important is to gain Knowledge of the Truth. This is possible not by merely following celibacy. Right thinking is required.

If alertness is related to the level of agitations in one's mind, how is it that some people who are highly materialistic and who must necessarily be having a high level of agitations are very alert, while some who are spiritually inclined are not alert?

It is important to define the word 'alert' correctly. Our alertness is related to our mind's interests. A materialistic person is alert to material things as they are in consonance with his interests. A spiritual person on the other hand may not be very alert in respect to material things but is alert to spiritual matters.

When there is a clash in our *dharmas* - such as one's *dharma* as a wife clashing with the *dharma* as a daughter or one's *dharma* as a career person clashing with his/her *dharma* as a seeker, which *dharma* should be given a higher priority?

There is no given rule relating to priority of *dharma*. Priority depends on the situation and would differ under different conditions. For instance, if the children have exams at the same time as the mother wants to attend a spiritual camp, her duty as a mother should come first and rather than attend the camp she should stay home with them. While doing any action, instead of feeling that it is being done for the husband, child or parent, offer the work as service to God. Then whatever be the work, we are in fact constantly fulfilling our *dharma* as seekers. There can be no clash of *dharmas,* if we do anything and everything with this attitude.

How do we get rid of bad habits?

Habits are not only physical ones e.g. smoking, drinking alcohol etc. but also mental ones such as short temper, jealousy etc. Most of us know of our physical habits but are not aware of our mental ones. If we are told that the glass of fruit juice we are about to drink contains poison, we would not drink it. The habit of losing temper is even more harmful than poison because it not only harms us but others as well. Most of us do not give up bad habits because:

a. We are not aware of them except when they are physical habits.

b. We compare ourselves with others and are satisfied that many others have bad habits and we need not be the only ones to give them up.

c. We are not fully aware of the consequences of our wrong actions, and

d. We enjoy indulging in our bad habits.

If we can live alertly and consciously, with an understanding of the need to give up bad habits, success will be ours.

Can you suggest some daily routines as *sadhana* (spiritual practice) for us?

Bathe as early as possible. This ensures the purity of the body and also prepares the mind by making it fresh for the morning spiritual practices.

The mind like the body also needs a bath. Spiritual practices like *sandhyavandanam (Gayatri), japa* (repetition of the Lord's name) *pooja,* (worship), *abhyasa* ((scriptural study) etc. serve this purpose. Have a morning routine and fix it time wise. Make it compulsory that is, without finishing it, do nothing else. Select a text and go through it at a suitable pace.

Then do the day's work as an offering to the Lord. After the day's work, say some evening prayers, also after bathing. Wash your feet before going to bed. Do not go to bed till you are very sleepy. Then glide into sleep with the Lord's name in the heart.

When are the duties of a householder complete?

Do not focus on the label of a householder. Look at it like this - when are the duties of a person complete? When we gain *prabala vairagya* (great dispassion), our duties as a member of one of the three initial *ashramas* (*brahmacharya, grihastha* and *vanaprastha*) are regarded complete. Then one may take *sanyasa* at once. It will not be wrong, for, the very purpose of one's duties is to gain such dispassion. This is the absolute answer from the highest standpoint.

Now, from the standpoint of our day-to-day life, as soon as one sees the face of one's first grandchild, our duties are complete. There is then no place for arguments anymore. Still if we want to stay, then that is our choice.

Ramakrishna Paramahamsa was married to Sharada Devi through child marriage, as was the custom in those days. When he became old enough to start family life, he was ready to go either way - live the life of a householder or adopt celibacy. He gave her the choice. She was a great lady. She chose her husband's path. They lived together and yet in total renunciation. Thus, wherever we are physically, we can be in mental *sanyasa* (renunciation). For instance, Tapovanji Maharaj did not have an iota of attachment even as a child. He was ever a *sannyasi.*

If a person is a social worker and empathises with the sorrows of others, is it necessary for him/her to do *upasana* (worship)?

A social worker who serves society with the attitude of serving God, need not do separate idol worship. On the other hand he/she should not have any insistence on not performing such worship. Social service will purify the mind qualifying him/her for the path of Knowledge. But if social service is not considered as God's worship, it may lead to pride. Also if society does not acknowledge the individual's contribution, it may lead to dejection. Hence for social service to be effective, it should be accompanied by Knowledge and devotion.

How far is there need for a seeker to read the Scriptures?

As long as the seeker has this question, there is need for him/her to read and be guided by the Scriptures. It is like asking how far is there need for a hungry person to eat. Sri Samarth Ramdasji says, "Once the goal is attained there is no need for *sadhana*."

First it is necessary to determine the goal and the means and then one should remain steadfast in the means adopted. Even after that there is a need to listen, read etc., to remove doubts and obstacles in the way. After experience of the Truth there is no need to do anything.

What is *prabala vairagya* (great dispassion)?

The answer our Scriptures give to this may be a little difficult to accept, because of the graphic used. When you throw up, do you examine the vomit, discuss it, etc? There is complete dispassion towards it. When we develop that kind of feeling to all the worldly joys, that is *prabala vairagya*. There is no harm in looking at or going through experiences but one who possesses such *vairagya* ceases to have any more urges for worldly experiences.

Ultimately it is not just a feeling but is born of deep conviction about what is Real and what is not *(nitya anitya vastu viveka)* and clarity about your goal in life *(mumukshutvam)*.

One can understand *Vedanta* intellectually, but it is very difficult to practice it in actual life, in real life situations. What should one do?

Understanding can be only intellectual. There seems to be a big gulf between what we understand and what we practice. The only solution is to 'do it'. If someone asks - how to get up early in the morning, the only answer is, "Get up"! One may set an alarm or arrange for a wake up call from the telephone exchange, but even after one is woken up one can just turn around and go back to sleep. One has to make up one's mind to get up and then, *do it.*

Further, real understanding takes place when it becomes a way of life; otherwise it is not understanding at all. If someone is sitting before a beautifully decorated *thali* of delicacies and is then told that one of the dishes, only one of them is poisoned, what will happen? Will the person try even one of those dishes? Will he say, "Intellectually I know it is poison, but the food is quite tempting?" Let me taste it and see for myself. After all, only one of the dishes is poisoned." Do you rationalise like this? Even if there is only a suspicion that there might be poison in it, we will reject it outright. Why? Our understanding of the consequences of poisoning is very clear. Temptation means death.

Our attachment to the physical body is such that only physical death scares us. We do not take mental death seriously. If we can see the hidden consequences, we will never be tempted.

Our *shantipaatha* says, *tejasvinaavadhitamastu*. May our life be brilliant, may our life be in accordance with our Knowledge. Only then it is real understanding. Our values must be seen in action.

When we want to give up identification with bad thoughts, and remain a witness to them, how do we go about it?

It is not sufficient that we are merely aware of improper thoughts.

This awareness must be accompanied by an understanding of the root cause of the wrong thought and its repercussions. As this understanding dawns on us, we can see ourselves receding from the wrong thought.

In *Vedanta* sometimes we hear, "Remove negative thoughts". At other times we are told, "Let thoughts come and go". How do we reconcile the two?

All spiritual instructions have a context with regard to a particular *sadhana*. Witnessing thoughts is suggested to the qualified person (with *chittashudhi* and *chitta naischalyam* - purity and focus of mind). If such instructions are given to unqualified students, they will never be able to witness their thoughts - they will run away with them! So for the unqualified or less qualified students, as part of the *sadhanas* to purify the mind, removing negative thoughts is recommended - in the initial stages.

It is said that ritualistic worship of a deity or idol is a step on the path to Self-realisation. What are the other evolutionary steps? Can one jump from one step to the next without attaining perfection in the previous one?

The first step of worship is *murti pooja*, the worship of a deity or an idol. Slowly one understands that the Lord who is being worshipped in that deity is not restricted to that form alone. He is present in the trees, plants, birds, animals and human beings also. Then the concept of worship changes to one of service. Watering the trees and plants is worship of God in that form. Feeding grains to the birds or food to animals is *pooja* to the Lord in those forms. Offering relief to the suffering and needy is God's worship in the form of human beings. Seeing the presence of God beyond the idol, in all beings, is a higher state of worship.

As one continues worship in this manner, the mind becomes purified gradually and the presence of God is felt all around. It is seen even in every particle of dust. This is a very beautiful form of *sadhana*. God is seen as the very core of existence in all things.

In living beings He is present as the life principle. Whenever anyone experiences joy, the Lord alone is present there as happiness. Thus a continuous awareness of His presence leads to higher levels of *sadhana*.

We come to the next part of the question, about jumping from one level of *sadhana* to another. While jumping, one may even break one's legs! Why should one want to jump? It shows impatience and a lack of readiness to take pains to put in consistent, arduous effort to achieve one's goal. We should be willing to do anything, follow whatever form of *sadhana* is pointed out to us (by the *Guru*). If we do it sincerely, swift progress is assured. Even if someone says that it is a long, tedious route, ignore it. Continue the *sadhana* and one will find that it becomes enjoyable. Slow and steady effort wins the race.

After the daily morning *pooja* what other spiritual *sadhana* should one do to keep oneself on the spiritual path?

The ritualistic worship that we do in the morning has a symbolic meaning. When we show *aarati* to the Lord, the light in which we see the idol, represents the light of Knowledge with which we see the Lord. In our Hindu tradition, after *aarati*, the plate with the lamp is brought in front of the devotees. We place our hands above the flame and then on our eyes. What does it signify? That the vision which we had just now, we take to our heart and then carry it with us. Usually, there is also some *chandan* (sandal paste) or *vibhuti* (ashes) on the plate - which we apply on our foreheads. In South India, men take some flowers or *tulsi* from the plate and tuck it behind the ears and ladies place it in their hair. The fragrance lingers and helps us carry the experience.

Each physical act in a *pooja* is symbolic. When the *pooja* is over, we are not done with it. We carry the joy and peace we experienced, through the activities during the rest of the day. We must remember that the Lord we worshipped outside is in our hearts also. The same Lord is in the hearts of all beings. This awareness should remain with us.

There was a great saint in India called Namdev Maharaj. As a young boy, he was told to perform the temple *pooja*. One day he was carrying the food offerings to the temple, when a dog suddenly snatched the *roti* (dry bread) from his hand and ran away. Namdev ran after the dog, crying and calling out. Someone stopped him and tried to console him. Then Namdev said, "I am not worried about the *roti* being taken away. I want to put ghee on it, because the dog may get a stomach-ache if he eats that dry *roti*." So God is not only in the idol. He is in our hearts and in the hearts of others too. This is the awareness we must carry with us.

Study the Scriptures, gain this vision and remain alert. In spiritual life the only *sadhana* is alertness. We forget very fast what we have to keep in mind. A man went to a doctor and said, "Doctor, I have two problems". "Tell me," said the doctor. "One is that I forget everything very quickly." The doctor asked "Okay, what is your second problem?" The man blinked "What second?" We are forgetful and careless. We must remain aware and alert, always.

Contemplation has been regarded as one of the hallmarks of old age. Can such an exercise have a negative influence on the individual?

This depends on the individual. Let us assume someone has a cold. On inquiring about it we are told that it is because of a change in the weather. But since such a change is universal, everyone in the area should also have been similarly afflicted. This is therefore because of the individual's weakness. For our part, if we introspect and find negative thoughts overpowering us, we will have to cleanse ourselves and discard these thoughts.

If one is not inclined towards rituals, then how can one intensify one's longing for Truth?

Each person has a different aptitude and mental makeup. We should follow the path suited to our personality.

The rational-minded should follow the path of enquiry (*jnana yoga*), the emotional - the path of devotion (*bhakti yoga*), the body oriented (*hatha yoga*) etc. None of us is hundred percent rational or emotional. But our predominant mental makeup should determine what path we follow. Start somewhere.

Some have starting problems - they keep asking, but never start. Others find it difficult to sustain their enthusiasm and interest after starting. Yet others get stuck with some practices and are unable to go beyond. A child was asked, "If you have two mangoes and I give you three, how many will you have?" The child said, "I don't know; my teacher always teaches me with apples". He was stuck with apple counting!... Right guidance will help us to start, sustain and go beyond all practices to reach the Truth.

Swami Chinmayananda only taught about *Karma Yoga*, *Bhakti Yoga* and *Jnana Yoga*. He has never touched upon *Raja Yoga*. What is the reason for this?

Swamiji would jocularly say sometimes that he only wanted to straighten his mind and not twist up his body! Each type of *yoga* needs a certain kind of aptitude and one need not take up something which does not suit one's aptitude when the goal can be obtained by other means which are more suitable to the individual.

5
HAPPINESS IS WITHIN

Vedanta teaches that the happiness that we seek from outside, is within us. We see that people are busy all day and night. They sometimes even say that they have no time to die! Everyone wants to go somewhere, to get something or to become something. Someone wants to become the Prime Minister, another, the President of the country, yet another wants to go to America. If you ask why they want to go somewhere or become something, they will say that they want happiness. To be or not to be something, to hold onto or to give up something, to meet and to part, are all for the sake of happiness alone. Marriage is for happiness and divorce also is for happiness. Man searches for happiness from outside all the time.

Vedanta says that the joy which each one is searching for is not outside, it is within. It even goes one step further and says, "You are that joy!" Our struggles end as soon as we realize this. We will be free. Manu says, "All that depends on another is sorrow: all that depends on one's Self is joy." Dependence is sorrow; freedom is joy. When we depend on things outside for peace and joy we get only bondage, not peace. There may be a fleeting glimpse of joy for a moment, but that is not true happiness; it is only an illusion of happiness. Real happiness is that which puts an end to sorrow.

There has been so called happiness in our life but that happiness has not removed our sorrows. So we have never been happy in the true sense. Only one who has turned his vision inward and realized the true happiness is no more bound. Once we contact this joy within, it can never be lost sight of, whatever the circumstances, time or place. From the experience of deep sleep we can understand that there can be happiness even when there is no object of enjoyment.

What is the source of this joy? It comes from the blissful Self alone - but we are unable to recognize it because of our ignorance of the Self. Our search along with the bondage ends when we gain this vision and realize our true nature to be Bliss.

We have seen people gaining comfort and happiness from material wealth whereas we have not seen the happiness and joy which people gain from spiritual wealth. How then would we get motivated to gain spiritual wealth?

It is not that we do not see the gains of spiritual wealth. It is only that we may not have been alert to an understanding that what we have seen is spiritual joy. A person who gains this spiritual wealth acquires equipoise, balance and serenity. He exudes peace, joy and love.

India is said to be a land of *rishis*. Then why so much unrest, poverty etc?

Problems are everywhere. Problems are there irrespective of the presence or absence of spirituality. Where are there no problems? For instance, the city of Jerusalem is sacred in Christianity, Islam and Judaism - yet see its state over the years and today. This is also seen with respect to so many other sacred and secular spots across the face of the globe. Wherever people have ego, desires, greed and so on, all these problems abound. This is not just true of India.

To whichever or whatever aspect of our lives we give priority, in that field or sector, we rise and vice-versa. This is true in all matters, not just spiritual ones. Take the instance of a boy who is academically bright but neglects his health. It may fail in time. We will be healthy only in those aspects of our personality to which we pay attention. Those to which we pay less attention will become weak. So even if we have the guidance of saints, Scriptures etc., only if we study them, focus on their wisdom and translate it into action, can we transform our lives. Spiritual strength need not always imply material prosperity, but if we strive for economic development, equipped with spiritual strength, there is nothing that we cannot achieve.

What advice would you give people on the threshold of old age?

At this stage in life, there is no time to waste. We have nothing to fear even if we have been consistently doing 'wrong'. The Lord's name is the panacea to all wrongs - the only antidote.

One has to accept the ways of the Maker and accept them without trying to fight against His judgment. Be prepared to die with no regrets or misgivings.

What are the right or wrong reasons to become a *sannyasin*?

First let us see what are the wrong reasons for taking the path of *sannyas* (renunciation).

a. *Sannyas* should not be taken as a form of escape. When there are a lot of problems at home, business is bankrupt or some tragedy takes place and we are unable to cope up with it, we think of running away and becoming a *sannyasin.*

b. Some take up *sannyas* for name, fame, power, pleasures etc., to head a big ashram, gain the respect and worship of people, enjoy pleasures without working for them or become known and famous. A person told *Gurudev*,

"Your profession is very good!" They think *sannyas* is another profession like being a doctor or engineer! When one takes *sannyas* as a means of escape, one again gets attached to some person or faces the same or different problems and suffers. If one does so for name and fame, again there is suffering if he/she does not get the desired attention. The same worldly attitude cannot give any peace of mind or bring about spiritual unfoldment.

True *sannyas* comes from a longing for Truth born of discrimination and dispassion. Having experienced the world and having ascertained its hollowness and limitations (*pareekshya lokaan karma chithaan, Braahmano nirveda maayaad*), one feels a longing for that which is eternal and decides to take to *sannyas*. It is then understood as a means to the Truth and not an escape from worldly duties. Such *sannyas* alone will bring great joy and spiritual unfoldment.

What is liberation or Self-realisation?

I shall explain through an example. It is always easy to understand the illustration but difficult to understand and apply the principle.

An award-winning actor was once playing the role of a beggar. His identification with the role was so complete that he began to feel he was really a beggar. He kept begging from others even after the shooting of the film was over. His colleagues took him to a psychiatrist, who realised that it was a case of mistaken identity. After the treatment, he regained his true identity and realised, 'I am an actor and not a beggar. That was only a role I had taken up. In fact, being (acting as) a beggar brought me a lot of money!'

Similarly, we are living in this world as finite individuals identified with our body, calling ourselves man, woman, rich, poor etc. *Vedanta* says that it is not our true nature. We are advised to, 'Drop our nature. Drop our identification with the finite and realise our Infinite nature as *Sat-Chit-Ananda*. Discarding our mistaken identity and recognition of our true nature is called liberation or Self-realisation.

It is better not to ask 'why did I identify with the finite?', 'which is the first birth of the *jiva*?', 'from where did the *jiva* come?' etc. Instead ask how can we be liberated? When a person suffers a bullet wound he/she does not sit to ask, "Who shot the bullet, why, from where, how?" The main interest is to get it out of the body and be relieved from the pain. Similarly, we find that we are bound by our ignorance and false notions. Do not ask how and why they came. Focus your thoughts and efforts in removing them and getting liberated.

We carry on doing our duties mechanically. We do not find interest in any worldly matters as we feel everything is an illusion. How can we bring interest into life and worldly matters?

Why are we not interested in worldly matters? Is it because our wishes are not fulfilled, or there is emotional dissatisfaction, intellectual frustration, non-recognition of our efforts etc.? Also, that the world is an illusion - is it merely, a repetition of someone's words or is it our own inner conviction? Are we philosophising because of disappointments or is the feeling genuine? Is our detachment born of discrimination?

If our detachment is genuine, then it is good. Then why should we again want to get interested in worldly matters? Why go backwards? March ahead. True detachment should give rise to a longing for the Truth and a desire for realisation. Once we gain realisation, we will do our duties with joy and enthusiasm, out of a sense of fulfillment - not as a burden.

However, if we are not ready for a full-time spiritual pursuit and we have understood that all is an illusion, then we must play our role in this world with interest. Enjoy the role; we have nothing to lose as we know it is only an illusion. An actor, knowing that it is only a role, plays it beautifully infused with interest and joy. Once, an actor died so convincingly in a play that his life insurance agent fainted in the audience!

How can one be happy when there is so much misery around? Is it not selfish to meditate and try to attain happiness for oneself?

When people around us are unhappy, it is our duty to help them out of their misery in whatever way and to whatever extent we can. The misery of others can be due to subjective or objective reasons. If someone needs money, we can help them financially. If they need emotional solace, we should provide that. Some need our time, so spend time with them.

We are not supposed to celebrate when others around us are unhappy. But again, that does not mean we should become or remain miserable. How can one who is himself unhappy alleviate the pain of others? A drowning man cannot be helped by one who does not know how to swim. How can a poor man help another financially? How can a physically weak man serve another in pain? How can an emotionally imbalanced person give emotional support to another? If we are trying to make money in order to serve the poor, or making ourselves physically strong and emotionally balanced in order to serve and give solace to others, it is not being selfish.

Serving others requires great inner strength. One hears of psychiatrists who themselves become patients or social workers who become bitter. So let us first gain inner strength and the right attitude; then we will succeed in alleviating the pain of others. Students in medical college should not give up their studies when they hear of disease around them. In fact, they must put forth more efforts to qualify as doctors because only then can they truly help others. Similarly, those who meditate to attain liberation are not selfish. They are only qualifying to liberate others later.

What is this freedom? In your lectures, you talk about attaining freedom, and point to that as the goal of life. Freedom from what? Are we not free people?

Ha! We think we are free? Think for yourself! We wake up in the morning and if hot water is not available for our baths, we become miserable. Then if we do not get the right cereal for breakfast, we are angry. At office, if the cleaner has disturbed the papers on our desk, we feel frustrated. When we get back home if the wife does not smile we get depressed. If she smiles too much, we are worried. See how delicately poised our happiness is? Where is the freedom?

The outside world of things and people is perpetually dictating our happiness and sorrows. We are slaves to the outside world and to our mind and senses. When we see some delicious chocolate mousse, are we free! Do not misunderstand. I am not saying do not have chocolate mousse. But do we have the mastery over our mind so that whenever we want to employ our mind or senses in a given field, we can do it; and whenever we want to stop and withdraw, we can? The freedom our Scriptures talk about is freedom from the slavery to our own mind.

We don't even know real worldly joy. When are we going to get *paramananda* - true spiritual bliss?

Understand this - worldly sorrow is a great joy as it turns us to the Higher. So, too, worldly joy is the greatest sorrow as it keeps us away from the Lord!

For most people, the one way for true joy is *Bhagawat smaranam-* remembering the Lord through His name. True joy is only with the Lord. Of course when we realise the Lord to be one with us, we may say that true joy is only in the Self. Know this now and experience great Bliss here and now.

6
TRANSCENDING EMOTIONS

In the Bhagawad Geeta, specially the 14th Chapter, we find a very good analysis of the mind. The mind is described as being constituted of three *gunas*. These three gunas are the climatic conditions of the mind. Just as the outside climate keeps on changing, so too our mental climate changes every moment. We find one moment interesting and the next moment we are very bored. Nowadays we understand *gunas* by the word 'mood'. We are given to using phrases like, 'I am not in a mood to listen', 'He is not in a good mood', 'You are in a happy mood', and so on. In Sanskrit there is a word *'moodha'* which incidentally means 'he who is under the control of moods'. Mark the similarity of the words mood and *moodha*!

In technical (Sanskrit) language, the three moods are variously *sattwic, rajasic* and *tamasic*. These moods or *gunas* have great influence on our mind; and their expressions are also many, but they can be easily understood. Since we do not know these *gunas* and their expressions we get carried away by them. The moods keep changing and we come under the influence of the one which is most overpowering at a particular moment. But if there is proper understanding of the play of each *guna* on our mind, then we can regulate them just as we regulate the volume of the loudspeaker.

When the student is highly *sattwic* there is complete communication and understanding. When the *sattwic* mood is disturbed by some *rajasic* thoughts, the mind gets distracted and disturbed, thus hindering the flow of wisdom. Our understanding is choked when *sattwa guna* is over powered by *rajas* or *tamas*.

These three *gunas* consistently play their games, influencing our mind. If we know the expressions and influence of the three *gunas* we can gauge our present mood and understand our mind better. Following the traits of *sattwa*, there will be more and more clarity in one's understanding of the world and of other people. If one follows *rajasic* traits, then the overpowering thoughts will hinder one's understanding; and if one follows *tamasic* traits then one cannot learn anything.

Having understood this, we have to conquer these *gunas*. We cannot get rid of them completely but their play on our mind can be checked and restrained. We can increase *sattwa guna* which will give us more clarity in our understanding. A man of wisdom or *gunatittah* is one who has transcended the three *gunas*.

As we grow older, we are tormented by the fear of loneliness, disease and death. How does one overcome these fears?

Fear is an integral part of life and tends to increase with age but it is only a symptom and not a disease. Vedanta has analyzed it and says: 'Fear arises at the empirical level from our attachments, our likes and dislikes.'

We dislike all that we are afraid of, like diseases and the loss of life or wealth. We also want to hold on to some other things and fear losing them. But the world is ever changing and transient.

The subtlest cause of fear is the alienation and the sense of otherness. All attachments arise from our attachment to people and things. The fear of losing all what one values and of getting afflicted by disease increases with age. A person who is free from attachments is unaffected by this. As Bhartrhari says, '*vairgya meva abhayaya*' (fearlessness is the result of a dispassionate mind).

What spiritual exercises would help overcome this fear - meditation or absolute devotion to God?

For atheists, spiritual vision is the only remedy. In the ocean, small waves are invariably swallowed by bigger waves. Suppose a wave knows it is only a form and its essential nature is water, then which wave can kill water? Big waves cannot swallow water and so cannot swallow small waves either. Fear is obliterated when identification with form is dropped and knowledge of the essence takes place.

What we generally see is only the appearance. But the Essential Truth is imperishable. This realization and acceptance of age as a natural process relieves fear.

Can creative activities reduce this fear?

I do not think so. How can creative activities help? While creative activities can keep a person's mind occupied for a while, the person will eventually succumb to fear. Only the right Vision and the Knowledge of Truth can render a person fearless.

It is said in the Upanishads that when a person accepts the 'Real Truth' he fears nothing. But the moment he strays form his path, his fears become alive and manifest.

Fear is the root of all impurities, desire and *vasanas*, says J. Krishnamurthi. What is your opinion on this?

Vedanta says that the root cause of all impurities is body identification, born from ignorance. When a person is asleep he does not have any body consciousness, body identification or attachment to the body. During that period neither does he have any impurities of desire, anger and so on. In the waking state all these impurities do trouble the ignorant person. A wise person has body consciousness but no body identification; hence he is free from all these impurities. Fear too is caused by body identification, resulting in foolish attachment to the body. Thus from this stand point J.Krishnamurti's statement is not completely true, because fear too is an 'effect' and not a 'cause'.

Rishis who have done *sadhana* are shown in our *Puranas* to have sometimes lost their tempers and given curses also. How can we explain this lack of control on their part?

The *Rishis* were at different levels of evolution. There were some who were only seekers and as a result of penance had acquired some mental powers. They had not acquired complete self-control or purity of mind and therefore misused their powers. There were other *Rishis* who had through their *tapas,* not only acquired special powers but also purity of mind. They cursed not out of anger but as a blessing in disguise for a specific purpose, as an act of purification. There were yet others who were totally in oneness with God. The curses of such persons were an expression of the will of God himself.

Is total detachment not difficult for a mother?

Detachment is difficult for a mother since motherhood is quite intense, natural and universal. So no one expects her to be indifferent to her children. But she is expected to use some *viveka* (discrimination) in her dealings. My mother had great *viveka*. After I completed the *brahmacharis'* course, my first posting as *brahmachari* was in Bhopal. My mother was relieved because it was not too far from home and also because I had relatives there. But my next posting was in far off Kanpur. Initially my mother was a little worried but then she came to terms with it beautifully when she told herself, "He has become the whole worlds"! She told me of this some time later. So to combine love, motherhood and discrimination is the idea and the ideal, and it is possible.

In the *Ramayana,* Kausalya initially objected to Rama leaving, saying, "The mother is greater than the father, even according to the Scriptures. I am saying, 'Do not go'." Then she realised that she should not come in the way of his *dharma paalana* (upkeep of *dharma*) and she let him go. No parent can ever be totally detached from his/her children but love can be combined with discrimination. This becomes particularly true if the son or daughter wants to become a *sannyasi* (renunciate), join the army, etc.

What is the difference between *vairagya* and *tyaga*?

Vairagya means dispassion. *Tyaga* means renunciation. If one has *raga*, attachment for things, one can not give them away. Even if asked one will say, "Ask for anything else, but not this." When there is *raga*, *tyaga* is difficult. It is not possible to give, renounce or sacrifice if attachment is present. *Vairagya* is a pre-requisite for *tyaga*. When Kaikeyi asked Rama to renounce the kingdom and go to the forest, he said, "Is that all? Why do you trouble my father so much for this? If you had just told me, 'Rama, go to the forest', I would have done it." If there is *vairagya*, *tyaga* is easy.

Most people are fearful of death. How can one learn to face death more confidently?

Fear arises only where there is attachment. Death in itself is actually not so frightening for us. It is death as a cause of separation from our near and dear things and beings that is frightening. If death meant that one could take one's wife and kids, house and servants, cars and money - I do not think that people would then be so afraid of death! The more we are attached to the outside world of things and beings, the more fear there will be of death. But if we are devoted to the Eternal Truth, then there is no question of any fear.

How to overcome anger?

Anger is a universal problem. People the world over suffer because of it - children, youngsters, adults, the worldly-minded and even spiritual seekers. Instead of asking about how to overcome anger, we should ask what anger is. Do not expect any readymade answers. We have to think about anger, understand what it does to us and observe the state of the angry and peaceful mind. Why do we get angry? Why do we want to overcome anger? And so on.

On enquiring, we understand that anger is dangerous; it harms us and others also. It makes us say and do things which we later regret. It makes us suffer. It reduces our efficiency and effectiveness. It gives us a bad name. A secretary said about her boss, "He never loses his temper. He always keeps it with him!"

Is this knowledge not sufficient to want us to get rid of it? Why should we carry with us something that is harmful and makes us suffer? Drop it, why keep it? Even a small fly or ant is instantly sprayed and killed or removed from the house. Then why keep this most harmful anger in the heart? May be we have not suffered enough because of it. If we did, we would get rid of it immediately.

Superficially we say, "Anger is bad; it makes one suffer, it does not help", etc. We do not mean it intensely. We can get rid of it only when our understanding is deep and intense. The example of the poisoned glass of milk will substantiate the point. When we understand deeply the harm anger does, and have great value for a peaceful mind, we will drop it instantly.

Supposing as you are about to drink a glass of milk, someone tells you it has poison. What will you do? Will you not instantly get rid of the milk? Even if there is no poison, a doubt created in the mind is enough. You will not drink it. Why? You have understood totally that drinking poison will cause death and you have value for life. You will not say, "Let me try, may be this once, may be it will not harm, may be there is no poison…".

Let us think. Why do we get angry? It is either when our ego is hurt, desires are obstructed, or expectations are not fulfilled. When our ego is pricked, we should, in fact, be thankful to the person for showing us our place in world. Think, why should the world fulfil all our expectations of it? We have expectations even from ourselves, which we are unable to live up to. When we are often unable to fulfil our expectations from ourselves, how can we expect the same from others?

No emotion is good or bad by itself. Anger is bad when it is for selfish reasons, when it is uncontrolled and when it enslaves us. What we should do is to elevate and divinise our emotions. Anger thus elevated cannot harm us; it can be of use to us. Instead of being angry when our selfish wishes are not fulfilled, if we direct our anger against injustice done towards others, or against unrighteousness or untruth, it will serve a purpose. Lakshmana got angry only when someone insulted Sri Rama. His anger was well under his control, and at a gesture from Sri Rama, he would immediately calm down. Also, when we redirect our anger from the world towards the Lord, we divinise our anger. The angry devotee says to the Lord, "Why do you not give me *darshan*? If you do not I shall never speak with You again." All our negative emotions, if directed towards the Lord, can thus be divinised. Ravana was finally liberated even though he had enmity towards the Lord.

How can one develop dispassion, especially when our attachment is very deep rooted?

What is the nature of attachment? To think that an object, being or relation gives us happiness, only that makes us happy, without it we are nothing and life is not worth living, etc. Strangely, even as we think this, we live on. Even before this attachment, we were living quite happily.

Bhagawan says that if one wants to overcome worldly attachments, one should get attached to a spiritually enlightened person who is detached from the world. He/she will be able to release us from all attachments.

a.   By attending *satsang*, all our false illusions are removed and we gain dispassion (*satsangatve nissangatvam…*). Think of life, life-style, value-system, and state of mind when we were not exposed to *satsang*. What did we give importance and time to? Now we realise things like 'I am wasting too much time in selecting clothes'. We develop a value for getting up early, attending spiritual camps etc. Do we not find ourselves getting detached from many things?

b.   Take up penance and vows. Decide to give up that which we are attached to.

c.   Think of the sorrow we experience because of our attachment. Is it worthwhile? Attachments cause fear, tension, jealousy, stress, anger etc. Attachments keep the mind preoccupied and make it unavailable for higher achievements. Attachment to the finite prevents us from attaining the infinite Self. Is that wise?

d.   All attachments spring from the attachment to one's body. We are attached to people, clothes, pleasures, comforts and name etc., all for the sake of the body. When the attachment to the body fades, all others automatically drop off. How to develop detachment towards the body? Do not pamper it. Look at the body objectively. It is a mass of filth, well-packed by the skin. We have to constantly scrub and wash it to keep it decent and presentable. Ascertaining its very nature will make us detached.

A man of detachment is happy wherever he is (*kasya sukham na karoti viraagah*). He is free and fearless.

7
DIVINE LOVE PURIFIES

To maintain an attitude of 'dedication to the Lord' at all times is
not easy and hence it should be cultivated through *bhakti*.
Alternately, when we act in a true *karma yoga* spirit we become
intimately aware of a Higher Presence guiding and controlling our
each step which kindles a desire to love the Higher - this is the
beginning of *bhakti*.

Supreme *bhakti* is achieved through *pooja, japa* and *chintan*
(contemplation) which are performed predominantly by the body,
speech and mind respectively. There are three aspects of the Lord,
viz. the Form, the Name and His true essential Nature as pure
Consciousness. We are advised to worship His Form with our
body, chant His Name with our speech and contemplate on His
true Nature with our mind.

To serve the whole universe itself as the manifestation of the Lord
is real *pooja*. We can cultivate this attitude initially by idol worship.

Japa is to repeat the name of the Lord. Mental *japa* is the best
which, when well performed is itself meditation (*japadhayaanam*).
Mental *japa* is difficult for a beginner and hence one should start
by singing hymns, followed by loud *japa* and then soft *japa* which
will culminate in the mental *japa*.

The mind thus purified by the *pooja* of the form of the Lord and
made single-pointed by the *japa* of the name of the Lord would
be merged in its source by the contemplation of the nature of the
Lord. Continuous loving contemplation done with an attitude of

Oneness with the Lord is the best. The strength of this attitude helps us us glide into supreme *bhakti*, which is pure existence - Bliss devoid of any attitude.

Are there any short-cuts to *moksha*?

A short cut is defined as the longest distance between two points: when one tries to take a short-cut in unknown territory, one may end up getting lost and taking much longer than necessary. The need to take a short- cut in spirituality is felt when one is lazy. There are no short-cuts but there is a relatively easy way to gain the supreme goal and that is by doing *japa* of 'His' name with *bhakt*i. Once you start walking the path that itself becomes the shortcut.

Can one do *Gayatri mantra* and *ishta mantra* together?

Do *Gayatri mantra* first and then *ishta mantra*. To store milk in a vessel, one needs to clean it first. *Gayatri mantra* purifies the interior of the vessel. With such a sanctified inside, one can fill one's heart with the *ishta mantra*. If one's *mantra* itself is *Gayatri* alone, stick to it.

The important thing is to practice or do it with total faith and love. This is the secret of success in *japa*.

Should one do *japa* sitting down or in and through the various activities?

Japa should be done sitting in one place. If we have guests in the house and we keep doing other things in between our conversation with them, is that a good way of greeting or treating them? So too with God, when we do *japa* we must give Him our undivided attention. This is possible only when we sit quietly in one place. But *nama smarana* (chanting or remembering of God's name) can be done anywhere and at any time.

It is said that *Rama Nama japa* alone is enough to attain enlightenment, as in the case of Samartha Ramdas. But it is also said that without the *jnana* conferred by the study of *Shastras*, one cannot attain *moksha*. Could you please resolve this contradiction?

Samarth Ramdas and other saints like him were also great *shastrajnas* (well-versed in the *shastras*). The seeker starts with *japa* and then *japa* takes over. When we become one with it, at the highest point of supreme devotion, the vision of oneness is revealed. In the *Bhagavad Geeta*, Bhagavan says:

Tesam satatayuktanam bhajatam pritipurvakam

Dadami budhiyogam tam yena mamupayanti te

Those who worship Me and are devoted to Me are blessed by Me with Knowledge.

Naradji told Valmiki to just repeat the *Rama Nama*. He did it sincerely and with complete faith and thus reached the Highest.

Some people can not do *japa*. They are very rational, intellectual and like to do *shastra vichara*. But after a certain point, when their heart is full with love, they drop that also. It is a question of *samskaras*. If we have *samskaras* of *shastra vichara*, start there; if we have *samskaras* of *japa*, we can start there. The main thing is to make sure that we start somewhere.

You say such profound things in your talks. But we are so old. Is there some injection that can give us a boost in our spiritual progress?

Our problem is that if we are given a difficult *sadhana*, we are unable do it (making excuses of old age and its attendant limitations) and if we are given a simple *sadhana*, we have little faith in its efficacy. Take the name of the Lord with total faith. That is the best thing at your age. In fact this is the best *sadhana* for every one at all times.

Q **How do we develop love for God?**

The only way is to seek the company of those who have deep love for God. To learn music one does not seek the company of a wrestler! One goes to a musician to learn, attends music concerts, reads about it, and listens to it more and more - one lives in that atmosphere. One has to keep exposing oneself to it. *Satsang* is the ideal way. Through *satsang* one comes to know about the glories of the Lord, His *nama* (name), *rupa* (form), *guna* (qualities), *dhama* (abode), *katha* (stories), *leela* (wondrous play), His absolute *swaroopa* (nature), *vibhooti* (glory) and His Knowledge.

A young man had great love for Krishna, because of His very mischievous, attractive and playful behaviour, whereas Rama always appeared very serious to him. He had reverence for Rama, but not love. Once he had to stay in Arya Vaidyashala in Coimbatore for a month-long treatment. He heard my cassettes on *Ramayana*. He told me that after listening to the entire lot of cassettes, he felt like embracing Rama! So, begin with doing *sravana* (listen). Then only a personal relationship is established and one develops intense love for the Lord. We see Rama as our friend, our master, our brother etc. Different people have different relationships with Him. Slowly the intensity generated in our heart grows. Then we do not need anything else. A little child does not want to leave the mother at all, but later on, even if the mother wants to hold him, he says 'no'. Thus love for God is a dependence that leads to independence unlike attachments to things and people of the world.

Q **Which aspect of Ramachandraji do you love the most?**

His love for the monkeys. Every aspect of Sri Ramachandraji is beautiful, but I love this the most.

Prabhu taru mul kapi dal par

The Lord is sitting under the tree and monkeys are jumping about on the branches. In His infinite compassion He raises them to His own state. See how Hanumanji could achieve almost anything. He should not be called a mere monkey. It is because of him that other monkeys are also respected.

Some people make themselves great by belittling other people, but Bhagavan's greatness is to make even small beings great.

There is a beautiful episode in *Ramayana* when Rama tells Vibhishana to take all kinds of clothes and ornaments in the chariot (*vimana*) and drop them from the sky. Then he tells the monkeys to go and grab what they can lay their hands on. In great glee, they wear the clothes and ornaments in all kinds of odd ways and preen themselves in front of Rama, demanding his admiration. It is said that he was so fond of the monkeys that even in *Krishnavatara* he continued feeding them.

So we should pray to Him, "O Lord, catch this monkey of my mind with the rope of Your love and keep the rope in Your hand."

If God liberates man in whatever emotion he approaches Him, as in the case of Ravana, then why is importance given to devotion for God?

Yes, it is true that God liberates all who think of him intensely and continuously, even if they do so with fear (Kamsa), enmity (Ravana), hatred (Sishupala) or passion (Kubja). However, remembering the Lord with love alone is great as:

a.   Even though Ravana and others were liberated, there was no beauty in their liberation. It only displayed the compassionate nature and the glory of the Lord. In the liberation of a devotee, there is beauty of both the Lord and His devotee. The greatness of the devotee invokes the grace of the Lord. Such devotees become ideals for others to follow.

b. When the Lord is remembered with anger, hatred etc., there may be intensity but the mind remains agitated and unhappy. In life, we see that whenever tragedy strikes, we are unable to remember the Lord. Even if we remember Him, we cannot put our heart into it. Even if it is intense, there is no joy in it. Whereas if we remember the Lord with love, we experience peace and happiness.

c. The devotee who remembers the Lord in love gets much more than liberation. The Lord Himself becomes his servant. Sri Krishna willingly drove Arjuna's chariot, and got tied up by Yashoda's love.

Bhakti is considered as both means (sadhana) and goal (sadhya). Please elaborate.

What is the goal of our life? All of us want peace and happiness. If we have name, fame, money, and power but no peace or happiness, it is all meaningless.

Now what is *bhakti*? Here we are talking only of devotion for God (*Ishwara bhakti*), not love for the country (*desha bhakti*) or devotion for the Guru (*Guru bhakti*) etc. When three types of thoughts - love (*prema*), respect (*aadara*) and faith (*shraddha*) combine, it results in *bhakti*. When true, abiding and unconditional *bhakti* arises in a person, what happens? He/she attains true peace and happiness - the goal of life. Even in ordinary love, when we think about, see or meet the person we love, we experience, though temporarily, peace and happiness. Then what to speak of supreme love for the supreme Lord! Man attains lasting peace and bliss. Hence *bhakti* is the goal.

Now, let us see how *bhakti* is the means. Pure love for the Lord can only arise in a pure mind. Presently our love for the Lord is polluted with many attachments, likes and dislikes. Love is the best means to purify the mind.

It is said that *karma yoga* purifies the mind. *Karma yoga* is the dedication of all actions done as self-less service at the altar of the Lord. There also it is the attitude of love and dedication which purifies. Therefore, *bhakti* (love) alone purifies. Hence it is a means.

Also, the pursuit of Self-knowledge is only possible when we have love (*bhakti*) for it. On Self-realisation, we experience our oneness with all beings which results in love for all (*bhakti*). Hence the path of Knowledge too has *bhakti* as its means and goal.

The *Tulsi Ramayan* says *saadhana saadhya raama paga nehu*. Both the means and the goal are love for the Lord on the path of *bhakti*.

On occasions like death, holy books like the *Guru Granth Sahib*, the *Geeta* etc. are read. It is generally seen that no one understands it or listens to it. Why do we read them? And what is the use?

We are told that we should study the Scriptures daily. Not just read but also understand them and with the right understanding, perform our duties and live a good life. In case we do not do so daily, for whatever reasons, concessions are made and we are told to study them, at least weekly. If even weekly is not possible, then at least on some special holy occasions or in some holy places. If not even then, at least when we are on the death-bed, some one should read them for us. It might encourage divine thoughts. Reading after our death can definitely not benefit us. However, those who read may understand the importance of regular study. On such occasions, people start thinking about their own lives and realise that they too will die one day and therefore their minds are more likely to turn to God.

Also, on such occasions, there is a lot of grief. By the reading of the Scriptures our minds are turned to God and we feel peaceful and consoled.

The instruction of reading the Scriptures is given for our benefit. We should therefore follow it. If we choose to ignore it, and read or listen mechanically, it is our fault. Therefore study the Scriptures daily, so we will understand them, and thereafter, reading will be a joy, and following their message, an even greater joy.

What is *pooja*? How should it be done? The Scriptures say that the Infinite can never be obtained by finite offerings. Then why should we do it?

Pooja means worship. Worship is of the Worshipful One. True worship is an expression of one's devotion, reverence and gratitude to someone from whom we have gained a lot.

Expression of devotion is not measured in terms of the material or financial value of things. When we offer something to express our love or gratitude, we say that it is a token of our love and appreciation. The token is not what is bought in the market for a few rupees or dollars. Our love is not limited to the price or measured by it. The one who receives the gift sees only the love behind the offering.

The *Shastras* say that the Lord is pleased more by the devotee's desire to worship Him than by the actual act of worship. An example will make this clear. A mother is busy cooking for guests. The little five-year-old child says, "Mummy, do not worry. I will help you." The mother knows how little help the child can give, but she feels very happy that the child understands that there is a lot of work and offers to help. She may even tell the guests that it was because of the child that she could finish all her work in time. When the Lord is pleased, we get everything. Hence worship, even though finite in nature, can take you to the Infinite.

Many people worship God so that their wishes may be fulfilled. They have desires and to whom will they express them if not to the One who can fulfill all desires? Here worship is not unconditional, it is not an expression of love alone; there is desire, perhaps for the removal of suffering, or else the gain of wealth, wife or children. The Lord accepts that also. In this case what they want is finite, but the Lord is pleased that they are at least recognising Him.

There is yet another category of people who do not want material things, but pray for purity of mind so that they can attain Realisation. Here again, the Lord is pleased and gives whatever is asked. It is the attitude behind the worship that really counts, not the activity itself. Attitudes cannot be measured in physical terms.

When the *Shastras* say that with the finite one cannot gain Infinity, what is meant is that on the strength of a *yajna* or *pooja* one cannot reach Infinity. It cannot be the result of an action, because action can only produce a finite result.

God is love and happiness. If God is everywhere, then why is there unhappiness in the world?

Air is everywhere, yet asthma patients gasp for air. Some are even known to die without air. The trouble is with the person, not with the air. Sunlight is everywhere, yet the blind person does not see. Even when the heat of the sun is felt, its light cannot be seen. Similarly, even though God is happiness and everywhere, because of spiritual ignorance we do not experience that. We are only repeating someone else's words that He is everywhere. Whatever glimpses of joy we experience are due to His all-pervading presence alone. Because of the veil of ignorance, man gets deluded and becomes unhappy *(Ajnaanenaavritam jnaanam tena muhyanti jantava)* .

What is the special meaning in Lakshamanji being on the right, Sitaji on the left and Hanumanji in the front of Shri Rama?

In our tradition whenever rituals are performed, the wife is always at the right of the husband. Whilst working or in the upkeep of *dharma*, she should be like his right hand. The human heart is more to the left. Sitaji is the seat of love and devotion, and is therefore at Shri Rama's left. Lakshamana was like Shri Rama's outer breath (*bahih praana*), always with him, his right hand, always supporting him, never opposing him (left symbolises opposition). Shri Hanumanji remained in the front, ever ready to serve the Lord at the slightest blink of His eye. Shri Rama, the Lord, is naturally the center of our life and is the focal point in the life of all His devotees (Lakshmana, Sita and Hanuman).

There is something inexplicable in *Ramayana*. Ravana participated in Sita *Swayamvar* and he saw Rama accomplish what he himself could not. Ravana said that none could kill Khara and Dushana, but they were vanquished single-handedly by Rama. Vali was killed and a bridge built across the ocean, impossible feats according to Ravana. Why did he still fail to understand Rama's true and divine nature?

Ravana knew everything. He knew Khara and Dushana's strength. He also knew that none other than *Bhagawan* could kill them. Yet his *ahankara* (pride) was so great, he was such a *maha-abhimani* (supremely conceited) that he could not accept it. His thinking was, "Only the Lord can kill them, but how can I be sure that this is only the Lord? I will test him and find out. If he is a man, there is nothing to worry about. I will just finish him off. If he is God, anyway he will kill me and if I am killed by God, I will get *moksha*. This surrender business is not in my blood."

On the one hand, Ravana had proof that Rama was none other than the Lord but, on the other hand, Rama ran after the golden deer, deceived like an ignorant man, not knowing that it was Maricha in disguise. So Ravana had his own doubts. When Ravana abducted Sita, Rama wept like any ordinary man and went around searching for her. Further, he took the help of monkeys. How could he be God, who is supposed to be omniscient and omnipotent?

Thus, if we see how Ravana's mind worked, we can understand this. It was because of his pride, arrogance and ego, that he had doubts though he knew things well. *Bhagawan's leela* is also very confusing. So he decided to go ahead and face things as they came. *Ramayana* is very beautiful if you study it in depth.

8
SPONTANEOUS AWARENESS OF THE SELF

Meditation is the effortless abidance in the awareness of one's true nature. It is the natural state of a realized person, a *jnani*. Having realized the nature of the Self to be Pure Consciousness, the Self of all beings, he is ever in that state of awareness. He is naturally and effortlessly established in the Self. It can be likened to the effortless awareness of being a human being. This is our natural state and we are aware of it in and through all times, effortlessly and naturally. This awareness is never lost. It is ever present. In the same way that we are aware of our human status, the *jnani* has the awareness that, "I am *Satchitananda*, pure consciousness, the infinite reality."

He is aware of this without a shadow of a doubt, disassociated by any vagueness or error. He abides in the awareness of his true nature, through all times of the day and night, through all periods of his life. As a waker, dreamer or sleeper the *jnani* blissfully, naturally and effortlessly abides in the awareness of the Self. Meditation is not an effort for him. He does not have to put forth any effort, for he now has nothing further to gain. He has experienced the Vedic declaration - "Everything indeed is *Brahman*, the Infinite."

For the seeker the word 'meditation' means practice of meditation. It is the repeated endeavour to restrain the mind from its habitual wanderings and establish it in the Self. It is the contemplation on the nature of the Self, by the Self. It is maintaining the thought of

understanding that, "I am Pure Consciousness," to the exclusion of all other thoughts.

A sincere, perseverant, patient and cheerful practitioner finally realizes *Brahman*, the infinite as his own Self. To such a *jnani*, the highest form of everlasting happiness becomes evident. It effortlessly manifests in his heart. He sees the same Self in all. He maintains an attitude of sameness towards all beings and objects of the world. It is expressed as supreme contentment and peace within himself and love towards all outside. He is totally fulfilled and never falls back from that supreme state.

Should meditation be done in spite of thoughts wandering?

Yes, sincere and consistent effort disciplines the body and finally stills the mind. Get joy from doing it.

What is the meaning of the *Mrithyunjaya Mantra* and how do we get maximum benefit from it?

Mrithyunjaya Mantra: *Trayambakam yaja mahe sugandhim pushti vardhanam, Oorvarukamiva bandhanam, Oorvarukamiva bandhanat mrithyor mukshiyamamrutat.*

Meaning; Just as when a cucumber is ripe it can be plucked off or it gets detached from the tree without any effort, in the same way release me from the fear of death (change) and make me immortal by freeing me from identification with the body.

This *mantra* is nothing other than meditation on our immortal Self.

What is the difference between *japa* and meditation?

Japa is a preparation for meditation. Meditation is abidance in the Self. For that one needs purity and concentration of mind, which one can get through *pooja* and *japa*.

A *Mahatama* once wrote that in order to go beyond the perception of one's limitedness, every day a *sadhak* should spend some time telling himself "I am the divine, eternal, unchanging, non-dual, absolute, substratum". According to him constant repetition of this suggestion will make it part and parcel of the *sadhak's* thought process. Is there any truth in this?

Definitely, there is truth in it. *Mahatmas* tell these things to *sadhaks* in their infinite wisdom based upon personal experience.

Could you explain the state of non-action of a Self-realised person.

To know that all action is taking place in my presence as Consciousness without any involvement by me is non-action. Action arises out of desire. To act without desire is non-action.

What is the nature of a *sthitaprajna*? What is a balanced state of mind? What is wisdom?

A *sthitaprajna* is one who is well established in the Knowledge and experience that he is the infinite Self, One alone without a second, appearing as this entire world. He is blissful and complete, not dependent on external factors for any kind of happiness or fulfillment. In the language of the *Geeta*, a *sthitaprajna* is one who is contented in the Self, by the Self and therefore, free from all desires of worldly things to become happy. When such a person performs actions, they rise from fulfillment and happiness. There is no attachment to the action itself or to any fruits of action.

Whatever results come, experiences that we call good, bad, pleasant, unpleasant, joyous or sad, through them all, there is equipoise of mind. This is the sign of a *sthitaprajna*.

As our mind gets purified, we gain glimpses of this Knowledge and we begin to understand many things. Even those who develop an interest in this Knowledge start losing their attachment to things and possessions to a great extent. Then you can well imagine the state of a *sthitaprajna*!

In Kathopanishad, Nachiketas is given three boons by Lord Yama. The third boon he asks is the answer to the question, "What is the nature of Reality or Truth?" Could you please explain it?

The nature of Truth is revealed as pure Existence, something which is not subject to birth, growth or death, and remains as 'isness' always. Then the question arises, "What is it that remains the same always?" The answer is *chit, chaitanya* or Consciousness. How? In our waking state of experiences, we have knowledge of many things. I am aware of 'a', 'b', 'c'…etc. The objects may vary, but Awareness does not change. Consciousness is always the same. In the dream state, the whole waking state is obliterated, but one is conscious of the dream. When one wakes up, the dream vanishes, but not the Consciousness. In the state of deep sleep we experience absence of everything, but we know or are aware of that absence. Consciousness is one and does not change, though we may go through different states of experiences. Pure Existence is this Infinite Consciousness. This is the nature of Truth.

Where is the Truth? It is all pervading but it is in our own heart, as our own Self. Now our attention is centered only on our body or mind and this Awareness is lost sight of. If we turn our attention to this Consciousness, we find that it is our own Self. It is me, myself! Realise that this 'you' is not just the assemblage of body, mind etc.

The Knowledge of the Truth, results in liberation. We are then totally liberated from all bondages. When one thinks that, "I am the body", one is naturally limited by the *dharma* of the body. If

one knows oneself as different from the body, there is freedom
from its bondage. The *Kathopanishad* teaches us the nature of
Reality, where it is and what is our relationship with it. "You are
that." This knowledge releases us from all bondage. In that very
instant, we are free.

What is the power of prayer?

Prayer is turning our mind to a greater source of power, knowledge
and wisdom. Once we are tuned up to the source, the energy,
power, knowledge, wisdom, etc. from there flows through us. For
example, when we plug in the fan, bulb, heater etc. to the electric
connection, the electric power flows through the instruments,
making the blades of the fan move, lighting the bulbs, making the
heater heat etc. Depending on the instrument, the power is seen to
manifest differently. Scientists tune their minds to Nature and she
reveals her secrets to them.

People are of different types and they pray to God in diverse
ways.

a. Those who consider God as a wish-fulfiller. They pray to God
    to fulfil their desires. If their desires are fulfilled, their faith is
    strengthened. If not there is disappointment and sometimes
    disillusionment or loss of faith. In such a prayer, there is a certain
    extent of surrender and therefore some calming of the mind.

b. Those who consider God as a well-wisher. They may also
    pray to God to fulfil their desires, but knowing that God is a
    well-wisher, they accept situations without disappointment if
    their wishes are not fulfilled. For example, a mother is a well-
    wisher and not a wish-fulfiller of a child. A child with fever
    may scream for an ice cream, but the mother will not succumb
    to the demand as it is not good for the child. Such people have
    greater surrender.

c. Those who do not ask the Lord for the fulfillment of worldly desires, as they know that He provides what is good for them without asking. They pray for purification of the mind, good qualities, right understanding etc. They naturally have greater surrender and therefore experience greater results.

d. Those who have tuned themselves to the extent that they have become one with the Lord. Their prayer is not in terms of asking anything but an expression of the Bliss they experience.

What is *moksha* (liberation)?

Moksha is *ananda swaroopa* (realising that happiness is one's own true nature) and *bandha* (bondage) is *dukha swaroopa* (sorrow). So *moksha* is freedom from bondage. This implies freedom from sorrow. There is nothing new to achieve but all *sadhana* is aimed at knowing who one really is. *Moksha* is renunciation of our false identity with body etc. and abidance in our true blissful Self.

Among the many *yogis* there have been very few *samsaris* and those few who were *samsaris* paid very little attention to *samsar*. Is this true?

Of the many *yogis*, some were known and some remained unknown. Since the lives of all *yogis* are not known one cannot give an accurate opinion on this question. But on examining the lives of those *yogis* who are known it appears that there is some truth in the above question. It is true that when a seeker develops an intense desire for Self-knowledge or God-realization, he/she cannot follow both worldly pursuits and spirituality, simultaneously. This is possible if the thirst for spiritual quest is feeble or after attaining complete Knowledge. Just as when one is intensely sleepy it is difficult to watch TV or read a book. After gaining complete Knowledge the person sees the whole world as divine and in his/

her mind there are no differences between worldly pursuits and spirituality and the dilemma ceases to exist. A wise person remains firmly established in the Supreme, even while working in the world. Samarth Ramdas says, "Live according to your nature, while recognizing the eternal within."

Q **A *jnani* sees God everywhere. Can we?**

We can. We start in the primary classes, with practices like prayer, *pooja* etc. Slowly we go higher and higher. A devotee used to go to the temple daily, chant prayers and return. One day he thought, "Everyday I say something and go away. I don't wait for God to say anything. I will listen today". He stood there. Mentally, he was still chattering. Then, slowly, he became silent, so silent that something happened. Thereafter he never went to the temple again. Someone met him in the marketplace and asked him, "What happened? You don't go to the temple anymore." He said, "I don't go to the temple because I see God everywhere." In prayer you speak to God. In meditation God speaks to you!